Investor Revolution!

INVESTOR REVOLUTION!

Overthrow Wall Street and Take Back Your Future

Thomas L. Hardin

International Standard Book Number: 1-933669-06-3
ISBN 13: 9781933669069
Library of Congress Catalog Card Number: Available upon request.
Printed in the United States of America.
This book is printed on acid-free paper.
12 11 10 09 08 07   7 6 5 4 3 2 1

This book is designed to provide accurate and authoritative information on the subject of personal finances. While all of the stories and anecdotes not otherwise noted in this book are based on true experiences, most of the names are pseudonyms, and some situations have been changed slightly to protect each individual's privacy. It is sold with the understanding that neither the Authors nor the Publisher is engaged in rendering legal, accounting, or other professional services by publishing this book. As each individual situation is unique, questions relevant to personal finances and specific to the individual should be addressed to an appropriate professional to ensure that the situation has been evaluated carefully and appropriately. The Authors and Publisher specifically disclaim any liability, loss, or risk which is incurred as a consequence, directly or indirectly, of the use and application of any of the contents of this work.

For information on publicity, marketing, or selling this book, contact Bryan Gambrel, Marketing Director, Literary Architects, 317-462-6329. For information on becoming a Literary Architects author, contact Renee Wilmeth, Acquisitions Director, 317-925-7045.

For information on the Canterbury Group or the author, Thomas L. Hardin, please call 317-732-2075 or 800-340-0234 or visit www.CanterburyGroup.com.

Also by Tom Hardin: *Never Too Old to Rock & Roll: Life After 50—The Best Years Yet*

www.literaryarchitects.com
www.investorrevolution.com
Cover design: Jill Broadhacker, Miller Brooks, Inc.
Interior design: Amy Hassos-Parker
Author photo credit: Don Distel
Contributing authors: Josh Green, Craig Overmyer, Gail Fink

Some glossary terms used with permission from Investopedia.com:
www.investopedia.com.

Some glossary terms used with permission from InvestorWords.com:
www.investorwords.com.

To my Canterbury Group Family
You are true Revolutionaries!!
Rock on!

Table of Contents

Preface

As someone who's been in the financial services industry for 30 years and worked in a variety of areas—in large and small firms, and with financial planners, investment consultants, and stockbrokers— I've observed that little has changed during that time. Most Wall Street firms are doing the same thing they've always done: trying to sell you products. They've used a number of different approaches over the years, but the result is the same—they sell, you buy, and they make money. As for you, well, who knows what the markets will do? After all, as the fine print says, past success is no guarantee of future performance.

In recent years, frustration with Wall Street firms and the development of new technologies like day trading and online investing have led many investors to try managing their portfolios on their own. They soon discovered, however, that they didn't want to spend their time watching the markets, studying charts, and trying to anticipate trends. Besides, they rarely achieved any long-term success.

If you find yourself nodding your head and thinking, "That's what happened to me," then this book is for you. *Investor Revolution* is for and about people who consider managing their own investments to be a burden rather than a hobby. It's about a new way of investing: a revolutionary way, which dispels the short-term performance myth and focuses on lifelong successful investing processes to achieve your long-term goals. If you're tired of the way Wall Street does business and you want a new model, you just may be ready to join the investor revolution.

Ultimately, this book is about finding peace of mind regarding your money. That may seem like a daunting task, but what is money, after all? I'm sure you've heard that it's the root of all evil, that it can't buy happiness, and various other clichés and definitions, but money is really about having the freedom and flexibility to do what you want to do. And we all know that few things cause more stress and concern than *not* having enough money.

The investor revolution is about trading financial stress for fiscal peace of mind—the secure feeling that comes from knowing you can put your kids through college, pay for emergencies, live comfortably, and enjoy your life. Not to mention enjoying the extras that money can bring, like travel, vacations, gifts, endowments, charitable contributions, and whatever else is important to you.

What This Book Is About

This book explores the anatomy of revolutions and shows why we're on the verge of yet another one—the investor revolution—as well as what it will mean for your future, and why you should join up! We'll take a closer look at what's happening in today's economy, including the impact of the aging baby boomers as they start reaching age 65. Most important, you'll discover a revolutionary investment process that will help you not only adapt to changing market conditions, but also be poised to thrive in whatever situations arise.

One crucial key to financial peace of mind is understanding risk and learning how to manage it. I'll tell you right up front—there's no such thing as a risk-free investment. Even if you were to bury your money in your backyard, where you could be pretty sure it would retain its value over time, you'd be subject to certain types of risk that you'll learn about in this book. No matter what markets, interest rates, and public opinion do, the real risk in investing has a lot more to do with psychological risk—switching products all the time, trying to chase hot stocks, and not having a flexible investment process that can keep up with the ever-changing environment.

Many people are afraid that one catastrophic event will wipe out their savings and ruin their future plans. They want certainty that their investments will be safe and their money will be there when they need it. The process outlined in this book was created to have the highest probability of not failing in changing market environments. You'll see how you *can* have your cake and eat it too—you can make more money and have less risk.

Traditional Wall Street firms don't have a process that is sufficiently dynamic to deal with our changing environment. Instead, they have a myriad of products that work in some environments and don't work in others, and they can't match them up. Their default position is to emphasize whatever worked best in the past environment.

We know that markets will fluctuate up and down, so we need a process that can benefit from the fact that markets do fluctuate. By trying to beat benchmarks and market indexes, Wall Street tends to promote what would have worked in the very recent past, causing you to be a victim of the short-term performance trap. This book offers a rules-based process that teaches you how to benefit from market fluctuation instead of becoming its victim.

Fine, you might say, but what are the rules? If you've read other books on investment management or financial planning, chances are you're confused by the many answers to that question. Book A recommends this approach, book B recommends a quite different approach, and book C seems to contradict them both. In fact, there seem to be more investment philosophies than there are investment managers.

There's no way to address all the theories advocated by others in the context of this book. However, the fact remains that most investors don't do as well as they should over the long term. Almost all well-thought-out philosophies and investment products have some validity. Each of them does well in certain market environments and then falls out of favor in other environments. The problems occur when the philosophy or investment product is out of favor. That's when you can experience large drops in principal and lose money.

This book advocates a radically different approach: a process that is dynamic enough to manage the many investment and risk-management tools to fit the ever-changing market. At the same time, the process needs to incorporate the individual investor's specific risk tolerance and long-term goals. Rather than following one style that falls out of favor, you'll learn how the revolutionary investment process focuses on lifelong performance and getting results. You'll learn how to evaluate potential advisors and crucial factors in choosing one, such as how the advisor manages your risk, and whether the advisor has a process for measuring and managing market fluctuation.

I urge you to read this book, consider what you find, and then draw your own conclusions. If it makes more sense than what you're doing now, you may be ready to join the investor revolution and arm yourself with the tools you'll need to thrive in the changing times that are coming our way.

Acknowledgements

To my Canterbury Group Family, Kim2, Sarah, Cheryl, Craig, Eric, Brad, Bennett, Gail, Jen, and David:

It's strange to have my name on the front of this book as "the author." I don't think any one person can write a book like *Investor Revolution!*. Revolutionary books require revolutionary thinkers—and lots and lots of research, brainstorming, and creative out-of-the-box thinking. Not to mention organizational and management skills, writing and editing talents, graphics capabilities, and the list goes on. It truly takes a village to write a cutting-edge book.

Investor Revolution! would have not have been created if it wasn't for my Canterbury Group family and several other professionals. I have many people to thank. The first two people I would like to thank are Sarah Billings and Cheryl Kahn. Sarah is the highest-energy person I know and was the project manager for *Investor Revolution.* Sarah was the hardworking taskmaster and competent organizer who drove the process to meet tight deadlines for this project. It was not rare for her to be working and talking with key players as late as 1:00 A.M., making sure everything was being done right and on time. Cheryl Kahn, the president of Canterbury Group, was involved with almost every aspect of the book. Cheryl did extensive research, and she did some of the writing and editing—and anything else that needed to be done. When we were down to the final crunch time, Sarah and Cheryl put their lives on hold to not only get the book done, but also make *Investor Revolution!* the very best it could be.

Next, I would like to thank my lead writer, Josh Green. Josh has an incredible writing talent. He gave up his summer to work on this project. You would not be reading this book now without the hard work and dedication of Josh Green. Gail Fink, who collaborated with me on my previous book *Never Too Old to Rock & Roll,* was a key player in the second stage of organizing the book and did the editing along with Renee Wilmeth. Renee and her colleague at Literary Architects, Bryan Gambrel, are true professionals and have done an excellent job as our publisher. Renee went well beyond what

I expected from her—to advise, edit, and generally hold my hand throughout the process.

Kim Dale, Canterbury's Director of Client Relations, gave important feedback and advice on the investment sections of the book. Her insights and advice have been critical not only to the book but also to the success of our company. Dr. Craig Overmyer, Canterbury's Director of Coaching, contributed valuable material for the Personal Wealth Management chapter. Investment revolutionaries Brad Herndon, CMT, CFA; David Vomund; Eric Zebrauskas; and Gregory Elminger advised on the financial chapter. I would also like to thank Tom Miller and the Miller Brooks team; Lorene Burkhart; Ingrid Cummings; Jim Haines, OD; Frank Hoffman, JD; Bill Martz; Patrick McKeand, Scott Quick, JD; and Steve Moeller, who all made important contributions to the content of the book.

Last, but certainly not least, I would like to thank my wife Kim for her unwavering support, advice, and love.

Tom Hardin
Indianapolis, Indiana

About the Author

Thomas L. Hardin, CMT, CFP®, is the CEO of Canterbury Group and the Managing Director and Chief Investment Officer of Canterbury Investment Management.

As Chief Investment Officer, Tom Hardin oversees all portfolio management and investment activity for Canterbury Investment Management. With more than 30 years of investment management experience and 27 years in personal wealth management and personal financial coaching, Tom is known for his creative investor education and revolutionary investment management process.

Tom has what may be the most diverse experience in the financial management industry today. After earning a bachelor's degree with a major in business from Skidmore College in Saratoga Springs, New York, Tom received his certification in portfolio management from the renowned University of Chicago Graduate School of Business. In addition, he has earned the following designations:

- Certified Financial Planner® (CFP®), 1982
- Certified Portfolio Manager through Hutton Portfolio Management, 1987
- Senior Portfolio Management Director, 1993
- Senior Investment Management Consultant, 1994
- Chartered Market Technician (CMT), 1997
- Chartered Retirement Planning Consultant (CRPC), 2002
- Certified Client-Centered Coach through American Business Visions, 2002

Tom began his investment career in 1977 as a Registered Representative of a New York Stock Exchange firm. From 1982 through 1986, he served as Regional Director of EF Hutton's Personal Financial Management Department, where he directed the financial and investment planning efforts of 32 branch offices and worked with some of the firm's highest income and net worth clients. Before founding Canterbury, Tom served as Senior Vice President and Senior Portfolio Management Director of Smith Barney's Portfolio Management Group.

Tom has enjoyed teaching and/or guest lecturing at:
- Purdue University's Krannert Graduate School of Business
- University of Indianapolis Business School
- American College in the Chartered Financial Consultant program (ChFC)
- AIQ Systems Conferences, the world's leader in artificial intelligence-based technical analysis trading software

Tom's first book, *Never Too Old to Rock & Roll: Life After 50— The Best Years Yet,* was published in 2005. He has written many newspaper, magazine, and professional journal articles, and he has authored several white papers. He has been featured in national financial radio programs and television shows and is a regular speaker on investment management topics.

Tom lives in Zionsville, Indiana, a suburb of Indianapolis, with his wife Kim.

Chapter 1

A Revolution
Is Upon Us

"For the times they are a-changin'."

—Bob Dylan

Bob Dylan was certainly onto something in the early 1960s when he wrote about the turbulent times and that they were a-changin'. The cultural revolution that began in the '60s was primarily about social and political change, two issues that engendered a great deal of passion.

Of course, if you stayed awake during fifth-grade social studies class, you know the cultural revolution was hardly the first American revolution. We Americans have a revolutionary spirit. Starting with the American Revolution that formed this country in the first place, our founding fathers and mothers launched us down a path that included battles for racial equality, civil rights, and women's suffrage, to name just a few.

You've probably noticed that the times, they are a-changin' again. Like the mass changes we saw as a nation in the 1960s, this next revolution will focus on something people are passionate about: their money and its effect on their quality of life. Investors who want to connect their money to their lives and their futures will drive this next revolution. Investors will totally change how they think about investing their money. And they will want to work with financial advisors who think the same way. This will be the investor revolution.

Investor: For the purposes of this book, anyone who has money invested. This term does not refer to a professional who invests money for other people.

This investor revolution will spur a monolithic shift, affecting life to a far greater degree than the advent of flower power and communal love. I'm talking about a new age in which we'll have greater opportunities available to us than any generation has ever had. Our next revolution will be driven by the largest investing generation to see modern history—the baby boomers.

As is true of all revolutions, those who see it coming will benefit most. The key is to understand and develop the know-how to take advantage of all the revolution has to offer.

Why are baby boomers the best generation to not only see the revolution coming but drive it and ride the wave of its benefits? Boomers are living longer. Sure, you say—increased longevity is a wonderful thing, but it raises some serious questions. If you live to be that old, will you have enough money to be financially secure for the rest of your life? Will millions of baby boomers leave the workforce at age 65 and expect Social Security to support them for 20, 30, or 40 more years? Have corporate scandals and a bear market caused irreparable damage to the future viability of counting on pensions and 401(k) plans? What happens to succeeding generations if Social Security goes bust, as many experts predict it will? Will our children have to shoulder the burden and support not just themselves, but an aging population as well? Can anything be done to ensure the future? Finances aren't the only area of concern. Can we stay healthy and vibrant as we age? What's our purpose in life when we're older? Will we have the freedom to do what we want?

We hear these questions from economic analysts and the popular media. Many expect our aging population to become a tremendous burden, overwhelming the healthcare system and becoming a drain on society. But boomers have a different course in mind. They plan to lead the next revolution.

Anatomy of a Revolution

These days, the words *revolution* and *revolutionary* are often overused or used out of context. Merely being "new" isn't all that sexy, so many marketing campaigns describe the latest products as "revolutionary" or "breakthrough." The word *revolution* loses its power when everything from car waxes to mop heads is touted as a breakthrough in modern life. But honestly, how exciting is a "revolution" that results in a shinier kitchen floor? I don't take the idea of a revolution that lightly, and neither should you.

In a real revolution, many things we believe and take for granted either change dramatically or become obsolete. A revolution involves momentous and complete change, such as when one government is overthrown and replaced with another. To understand exactly how a revolution works, let's look a little more closely at the American Revolution, because it provides a familiar example. I've observed that successful revolutions seem to go through four stages.

During the first, or creative stage of revolutions, a new idea causes a rethinking process. For example, Thomas Paine's pamphlet *Common Sense* challenged the authority of the British government. As the first work to openly ask for American independence, it showed that the colonists were questioning their status quo and coming up with creative ideas to do something about it.

The second stage in a revolution—the innovative stage—occurs as the new idea gains mainstream awareness, begins to conflict with established thoughts and practices, and eventually causes a polarization of opposing points of view and innovative actions. In the American Revolution, the concept of independence soon resulted in innovative acts of defiance like the Boston Tea Party.

The third step, or growth stage, occurs when the revolution reaches critical mass, meaning that enough people buy into it to start effecting change. During this stage, outright conflict often erupts, and the battle begins. In the case of the American Revolution, this stage took place when British troops arrived, militias were mustered, and opposing armies squared off on the battlefield. Bear in mind, not everyone buys in at the beginning of the growth stage.

Even in the American Revolution, there were loyalists who did not agree with the move toward independence.

The last stage, or maturity stage, occurs when the revolutionaries win the fight and transform to the new model. At this point, the revolutionary idea has become "the way."

Four Stages of a Revolution

1. *The creative stage*: A new idea or technology causes a rethinking process.

2. *The innovative stage*: The new idea gains mainstream awareness, begins to conflict with established thoughts and practices, and eventually causes a polarization of opposing points of view.

3. *The growth stage*: The revolution reaches critical mass. Conflict erupts, and the battle begins.

4. *The maturity stage*: The revolutionaries win the fight and transform to the new model.

Ages and Stages

Because our American Revolution exemplifies the progression of a revolution, we can look back in history and see how these characteristics have applied across the ages. Eras and ages have all been marked by revolution. And revolution in turn has driven the progression of the age.

The Stone Age ended with the development of agriculture, the domestication of animals, and the discovery of bronze. The last of these pushed the masses to further creations and resulted in the dawning of the Bronze Age, a period that saw advanced metalworking. During the Bronze Age, we can be reasonably certain that someone embraced the revolution of this newfangled metal while the establishment was still entrenched in stone. The global spread of metalworking resulted in new developments that led to the end of the Bronze Age and the beginning of the Iron Age. For those periods in history, the creation, growth, and distribution of metal caused revolutionary changes in human evolution.

The Renaissance of the fifteenth century represented a revolution in the dissemination of knowledge brought on by the discovery of printing. The Age of Enlightenment was also revolutionary in intellectual movement and established the framework for the American Revolution and the rise of capitalism. The Age of Discovery from the fifteenth to seventeenth centuries overlapped the Renaissance and Enlightenment Ages and allows us to see how innovations in one area can trigger creativity and breakthroughs in a different direction, thus causing multiple revolutions across a time span with equally explosive results. For example, the revolution in physics during the Age of Discovery emboldened Enlightenment thinkers to apply a systematic way of thinking to human activity.

Many of us are familiar with the results of the Industrial Age. The Industrial Age rested on three major developments. Most important was the completion of the nation's modern transportation and communication networks—railroad, telegraph, steamship, and cable—which made possible the high-volume flow of goods essential for the creation of modern industrial economies. The second was the advent of electricity in the 1880s, which provided a more flexible source of power than steam; new means of urban transportation (the trolley and the subway); and brighter, cheaper, and safer illumination in factories, offices, and homes. The third development was the beginning of the application of science to industrial processes and to the creation of new and improved consumer and industrial products.

Age: A period in the history of humankind marked by a distinctive characteristic or achievement.

Revolution: A sudden or momentous change in a situation.

Like the Bronze and Iron Ages, the Industrial Age was preceded by a technological revolution—the Industrial Revolution—when the mass adoption of factories and equipment changed everything from how goods were produced to how and where people lived. In the years between the World Wars, the primary engine of economic growth and transformation was the automobile industry; after World War II, it was the computer. The impact of these technologies was profound.

As the Industrial Revolution gained steam (literally), it resulted in the mass production of cars and then airplanes. But mass production was only part of the Industrial Revolution. States and the federal government built roads—including a national interstate highway system. As airline travel grew, towns and cities built airports, allowing airline companies to expand their carrier routes. People were more easily able to travel from one place to another. This skyrocketing mobility changed the business world almost immediately, as travel rapidly grew to include everything from international journeys to the daily commute.

The Industrial Revolution also meant that people weren't likely to die within 15 miles of where they were born, as was probably the case in the simpler Stone Age. Some people living in the Industrial Age didn't even work within 15 miles of home: Suburbs rippled out from cities because businesspeople could drive from home to work and back again, opening the door for all types of entrepreneurial possibilities.

The Space Age also made important contributions to society. Spanning from 1957 to the 1990s, most people would agree this age greatly influenced the political, scientific, and technological achievements of this short but revolutionary time, which also overlapped the Industrial and Information Ages.

The Information Age began around 1970, and it was noted for the abundant publication, consumption, and manipulation of information. The Information Age picked up serious momentum in the 1980s, after the launch of the first IBM personal computer in 1981 and the growth from 4 to more than 300,000 Internet hosts in the twenty years from 1970 to 1990. It didn't take long for the Internet to become a tool that most businesses can't function without. Instead of roads and interstates, our newest path to the future became the information superhighway. We are still appreciating the impact of this current age, while recognizing the revolutionary impact it has already had.

The Rise and Fall (and Rise) of Napster

The Information Age created many technological advances that grew into successful business ideas. Although it can be argued that there are revolutions and revolutionary systems in the world of technology every day, in order to examine a full cycle more closely, we chose an example that many will remember: Napster's peer-to-peer file-sharing program. It was, at the time, considered by many to be revolutionary in its potential to force the music industry into a new way of doing business; and, in the long term, many will say the early battles Napster fought became the basis for what is now a file-sharing revolution driven by MP3 players like the iPod. Napster provides a good example of the anatomy of a revolution.

Before the ubiquity of broadband data connections, users had to move files around via e-mail (or disks), and file size was an issue—especially for audio or sound files. Enter the MP3 file format. Created by the German company Fraunhofer Geselltschaft (FhG) in 1989, this format compresses audio to enable easier transfer. The files are still big, but users can record or save an entire three-minute song in an easy-to-trade file.

As computers handling multimedia and networking software at home became the norm, the average American—especially technically savvy kids—figured out that it's pretty easy to pull and save data from a commercial CD. That meant they could not only play their music CDs (which had been around since the mid 1980s) on their computers, but also scan, manipulate, and record them. More important, they could trade individual songs with other users via the Internet. But audio files—even MP3s—were big, sometimes too big to e-mail back and forth.

In 1999, an 18-year-old Northeastern University dropout named Shawn Fanning created a free peer-to-peer file-sharing program specifically for music MP3s. If you were a Napster user, all you had to do was download the Napster software program to your computer, which then connected to Napster's central servers and told them which files were available on your machines. Meanwhile, you and all the other Napster users could access each other's file directories and download music directly from each other's computers. No files were stored on Napster's central servers, just a directory containing a complete list of every shared song available on every computer connected at the time.

Napster was an unthinkable concept only a few years before that point, but with its creation, entire songs and CDs could be downloaded at no cost to the consumer. It took a single revolutionary to apply the preexisting peer-to-peer file-sharing technology to music MP3s and establish a virtual meeting point for music enthusiasts.

In just a few months, Napster had record industry executives tossing and turning all night long, rethinking entire marketing and distribution strategies and everything they had previously known about the industry. Suddenly, their model had changed. Music lovers who up to that point had been required to buy an entire CD to get one song they liked could now go to Napster, find the song, download it, and create their own CDs of their favorite songs—all for free. Terrified, music industry executives saw Napster as a revolution that would render the traditional model obsolete.

During any good revolution, you can either fight it or join in. Although music industry executives fought and won a lawsuit against Napster and other file sharers for copyright infringement, many are now jumping on the file-sharing bandwagon. The industry is adapting and starting to market fee-based services like iTunes to make up for lagging CD sales.

The Keys to the Napster Revolution

There were two keys to the Napster revolution. First, the technology existed to support it. A calculated byproduct of the Information Age, it came about because of the invention of the computer. From the computer, we were introduced to the PC, software, and companies like Microsoft that showed us how computer technology could streamline our businesses and our lives. The availability of computers made it possible for Internet usage to develop at a breakneck pace, and it soon became a luxury most consumers couldn't live without.

The technology for listening to music followed a similar path, as radios, record players, and eight-track players became yard-sale items. With the advent of CDs and MP3 players, people found that pulling music from these media and posting it on the Internet could be a great way to share their collections. Better yet, peer-to-peer file sharing let people access each other's computers and download files directly.

However, that's just one key to the revolution. The second reason Napster became a huge success was not only that the technology existed, but also because *consumers really wanted it.*

Recap: The Four Stages of the Napster Revolution

At the beginning of this chapter, you learned the four stages of a revolution, and they all apply to the Napster revolution. The first stage, the creative stage, happens when a new idea or technology creates a rethinking process. In this case, the existence of peer-to-peer file sharing and the demand for fast, affordable music downloads led Shawn Fanning to develop the Napster software program.

In stage two, the innovative stage, the new idea gains mainstream awareness and begins to conflict with established thoughts and practices. When Shawn Fanning uploaded his original beta version to download.com, it quickly became one of the hottest downloads on the site.

Stage three, the growth stage, should be fairly obvious: In less than a year, Napster went from zero to 60 million visitors per month. The revolution quickly reached critical mass and faced staunch opposition from the music industry. Conflict erupted, and Napster lost the first skirmish but eventually prevailed and went on to win the war. Today, in its maturity stage, Napster and other programs like it legally offer unlimited access to CD-quality music and transfer of MP3 files to computers and MP3 players.

Widespread access to the Internet, along with multitudes of music lovers fed up with paying high prices for a standardized and outdated music-delivery system, drove the Napster revolution and showed that customization through consumer revolution and demand was possible. Today's savvy consumers are using the plentitude of information to buck traditional approaches in all facets of our lives. Everything from the way we like our coffee to our views on retirement and our investment strategy is undergoing a serious change. We have the ability to paint the perfect picture for our lives and customize the means to live it.

What's Next on the Horizon?

One of the results of the Industrial Revolution was the ability to mass produce. With this mass production of products came a revolutionary distribution model that favored the product-push approach and relied on sales and advertising. Salespeople were paid commissions and markups to sell products by creating a need in clients' minds or giving them what they thought they wanted, even if it wasn't the best choice for them. This business model made getting objective advice next to impossible. The proliferation of so many choices resulted in overload, leaving consumers confused and looking for a better model than the product-push.

Developments from the Space and Information Ages have added to this overwhelming situation. But what can we build for ourselves with all this information, and where will this highway take us? What will come next? Our choices have become so great that it's important to have a trusted advisor or consultant to understand our needs and help match them to a specific product or choice. This consultative-based model focuses on demand-pull rather than product-push. It looks for customized solutions to our individual needs and a dynamic process that can sift through the myriad of choices and ultimately come to the result that's best for us.

As we discuss the entrenched culture and business models in the financial sector, remember what it takes to be revolutionary. The easy access to information leads to creative new ideas; new ideas lead to new innovations; and new innovations lead to revolutions. The investor revolution will occur as converging factors on the edge of exploding allow us to more effectively control our money and experience our lives as we want to today.

Chapter 2

Aging, Boomers, and the S-Curve

"Nothing is so intolerable to man as being fully at rest, without a passion, without business, without entertainment, without care."

—Blaise Pascal, seventeenth-century philosopher

When we think of what we know about investing, we think about what we learned from our parents and grandparents. Former news anchor and author Tom Brokaw called them "the Greatest Generation," and he was right. They overcame real adversity. They spent their youth in the Great Depression, growing up in an era of scarcity and learning what it feels like when there's not enough to go around. That awful period was followed by something even worse: World War II. And just when this generation thought everything was going to be okay, they faced a new era of modern technology and the Cold War. There were new homes, cars, and appliances along with new jobs, families, and modern stress levels.

Think of what the world and society would look like today had it not been for the sacrifices of the Greatest Generation. Their experiences made the world a better place but left a lasting and important impression on them—and, as a result, on us, too. Change was something this steady generation didn't embrace because, to them, change usually meant hardship.

HeadlightVision, Ltd., a London-based research consultancy company, studied more than 40,000 people between the ages of 45 and 75 from the United States, the United Kingdom, Italy, Spain, Japan, and Sweden. The study identified the core values and characteristic behavior of three separate groups, including the one we know as the Greatest Generation. HeadlightVision calls them *Stoic Seniors* and identifies them as people born between 1926 and 1935. Not surprisingly, this group tends to be cautious, conservative, and conscientious with a strong sense of family duty. They're usually thrifty, even when affluent, and they respect sacrifice. They "make do" and make the best of what they have. They pay their bills promptly and dislike surprises.

After living through a depression, a world war, and the dawning of the atomic age, it's no wonder the Greatest Generation developed those traits and behaviors. They grew up believing conditions were bad today and could be worse tomorrow. This group wasn't crazy about change, and they looked forward to a quiet, stable future. They weren't as concerned with revolutionizing as they were with enduring.

On April 3 and 4, 1974, a massive storm swept the United States, with 148 vicious tornadoes leaving 330 people dead and a 2,500-mile path of destruction. The state of Kentucky was ravaged by 26 tornadoes, making it the worst storm disaster in the state's history. In Louisville, where I lived at the time, houses were knocked down, and the convention center's roof was blown off. The whole city looked as if it had been destroyed—a familiar sight to those used to seeing Hurricane Katrina video footage from New Orleans in 2005. For the next year or so, every time there was a big storm, those of us who lived in Louisville headed for our basements; that day of tornadoes had left its mark. After enduring just a few months of worry, I can only imagine how the Greatest Generation felt after bearing years of adversity.

For many people, growing up during the Great Depression resulted in low expectations, conservative thinking, and an unwillingness to spend a lot of money. "Waste not, want not" became their mantra. Voluntary career changes were unheard of, and most workers were employed by the same company throughout their working years. Not surprisingly, the concept of retirement took root in that generation. Prior to the Great Depression, the majority of Americans didn't believe government should care for the aged, disabled, or needy. After the Depression, those attitudes changed. Many workers had learned firsthand that they could suffer from events over which they had no control, and they looked to the government for help and protection.

With the development of Social Security in 1935 and its expansion over the subsequent years, Americans began working forty, fifty, or sixty hours per week. Working hard allayed their fears, but it resulted in an out-of-balance lifestyle. As a result, people looked forward to retiring to something completely opposite and equally out of balance—forty to sixty hours of leisure time each week, when many went from overwork and overstress to a life of absolute boredom.

Growing up under drastically different circumstances, the next generation embraced a different set of values and behaviors. HeadlightVision describes people born between 1936 and 1955 as liberal, socially tolerant individuals with a live-for-the-moment attitude. Determined to stay young and redefine middle age, this group has a greater desire for balance between work and life. Using the prior generation as role models for aging won't work for this group. Luckily for us, a better alternative lies within our midst, in the oldest segment of the baby boom generation.

Birth Waves and the S-Curve

According to the U.S. Census Bureau, baby boomers include everyone born from 1946 through 1964. People in the financial arena have a slightly different take on the term baby boom. In the stock market, a boom refers to the span of time between the bottom and the top of a market, or between the trough and the peak. In other words, it's a period of explosive growth. A boom ends when the market begins to flatten out and then decline again. Therefore, the real baby boom—or what I call the rock-and-roll generation—extended from 1937 through 1957.

Boom: A period of higher-than-average growth in the stock market, economy, or other sector. The term refers to explosive growth.

If you look at twentieth-century population growth, it's easy to see where the true boom occurred. It consisted of three clear-cut surges or waves: 1937 to 1944, 1945 to 1949, and 1950 to 1957. After 1957, the growth rate flattened out and then began to decline. (See figure 2.1.)

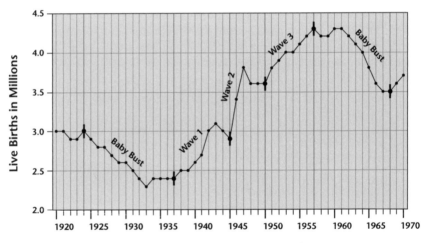

FIGURE 2.1 Twentieth-century population growth

Now, let's take a closer look at the significance of the three birth waves. In his book *The Great Boom Ahead* (Hyperion, 1993), Harvard economist Harry S. Dent described the typical development cycle, or S-curve, of a new product (see figure 2.2):

> *All new products and technologies go through three clear stages of growth.... It takes the same time for a new technology or product to go from 0 to 10 percent (innovation phase) of its potential market as it does from 10 to 90 percent (growth phase) and as it does from 90 to 100 percent (maturity phase)."*

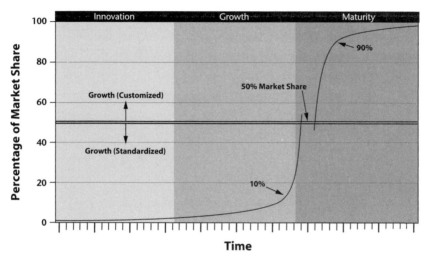

FIGURE 2.2 Typical S-curve

Dent used the development of the automobile to illustrate his point. When the first automobiles appeared in the late 1890s and early 1900s, no one took them seriously. People laughed at the "horseless carriages" and considered them toys for the rich rather than serious transportation. By 1914, at the end of the innovation phase, only 10 percent of urban families could afford to buy a car.

In 1914, Henry Ford developed a standardized design of the Model T. Ford's revolutionary assembly line process made it easier, more efficient, and less expensive to manufacture his cars. Despite the fact that buyers had no choice in make (Model T) or color (black), the cars sold like hotcakes. Because of the cars' price and accessibility, consumers were willing to overlook the fact that they had no choices.

This idea of standardization marks the beginning of a growth phase, which consists of two equal segments: standardization and customization. As Dent explains, it takes as long for a product to go from 10 to 50 percent of the potential market (standardization) as it does to go from 50 to 90 percent (customization). Ford's moving assembly line refined the process for building high-quality, standardized cars. Seven years later, in 1921, roughly 50 percent of urban families owned cars. That's when General Motors began customizing cars by offering different models and colors. Seven years after that, in 1928, the growth phase ended, and 90 percent of American families owned automobiles. (See figure 2.3.)

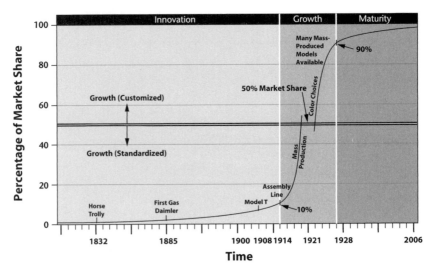

FIGURE 2.3 Model T S-curve

Standardize: To bring to or make of an established standard size, weight, quality, strength, or the like.

Customize: To modify or build according to individual or personal specifications or preference.

After 1928, the automobile industry entered the maturity phase. Cars were accepted as part of American society. Installment financing and automobile-related industries swept the country, making the twentieth century, in Dent's words, "the century of the car." Today, when we buy cars, we have an almost infinite number of choices—from engines to upholstery to electronic accessories. Car manufacturers spend as much time designing the cup holders as the drive train. We've entered the maturity phase.

Figure 2.4 shows an S-curve applied to the rock-and-roll generation's birth waves.

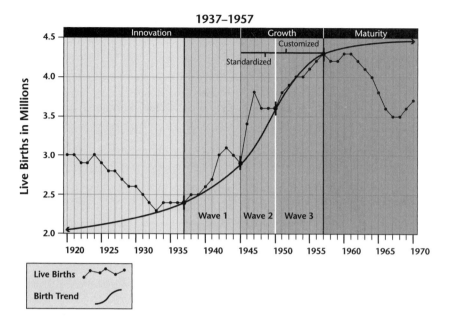

FIGURE 2.4 The Real Baby Boom

Interestingly, Dent's three phases—innovation, growth, and maturity—also apply to the rock-and-roll generation, their coming of age, and the ensuing cultural revolution. If we apply Dent's S-curve to the age ranges the U.S. Census Bureau provides for the baby boomers' birth years, you'll see three clear breaks. The early range falls into the innovation phase, the middle group falls into the growth phase, and the final group falls into the maturity phase.

The Innovation Phase (Born Prior to 1945)

Because of low birth rates during the Depression, people born in 1938 and 1939 had a radically different outlook from people born just a few years earlier. The preceding "baby bust" generation, born from 1926 through 1933, was very small. Those kids grew up during the Depression and World War II—cataclysmic events that dramatically affected their personalities. In contrast, the earliest rock-and-rollers grew up in the 1950s and came of age socially in the early 1960s. They grew up during relatively good economic times and were too young to remember World War II.

Unfortunately, those first rock-and-rollers had a major identity crisis of their own. As youth, they had no real role models because their upbringing and early life experiences were vastly different from those of the previous generations. This group was fragmented, with many ideas about who and what they could be, but no consensus. However, just as the development of the automobile assembly line led to the transportation revolution, the rock-and-rollers' search for identity eventually led to the cultural revolution of the 1960s.

Almost without exception, the leaders of the cultural revolution were born prior to 1946. These role models included personalities as diverse as Malcolm X, Hugh Hefner, Martin Luther King, Jr., Gloria Steinem, and Muhammad Ali. In the popular arts, first-phase innovators included Andy Warhol, Elvis Presley, Buddy Holly, Peter Fonda, Bob Dylan, Joan Baez, Jimi Hendrix, Janis Joplin, Jim Morrison, John Denver, "Mama" Cass Elliott, and Mick Jagger. Although you may disagree with some of their radical ideas, these individuals were agents of change, and their contributions were immeasurable.

The Growth Phase (Born 1945–1957)

This second group endorsed and spread the cultural revolution started by the innovators. They jumped on the bandwagon (or, in their case, the Volkswagen bus) and caused the movement to grow and evolve. Although they weren't the innovators, members of the growth phase had greater impact (and often receive all the credit) because their numbers dwarfed the previous group's. Take Woodstock, for example. Most people consider the 1969 music concert and festival to be the coming-out party of the baby boom generation. The real leaders, though—almost all the performers appearing on stage—were born during the innovation phase prior to 1945.

As Dent observed, the growth phase consists of two parts: standardization and customization. When applied to the rock-and-roll generation, the standardization segment occurred when those born between 1945 and 1950 came of age. With their long hair, bell-bottom jeans, wide belts, and tie-dyed T-shirts, many in the standardization group seemed to have come from a single mold. They spoke the same language ("Far out, man") and thought the same thoughts. They were anti-war, anti-establishment, and pro-peace. It didn't matter if they were wealthy or poor, college educated or high school dropouts; their ideology was the same: Peace and love! Sex, drugs, and rock and roll! They knew how to dress and which records to buy because their style was predetermined for them; they simply followed the innovators' lead.

However, like any other group of product adopters, many members of the rock-and-roll generation didn't buy into the new culture. Just as only half of all car buyers owned Model Ts during the standardization segment of the automobile's development, only about half the people born during this birth wave participated in the cultural revolution during its standardization segment. The other half retained values similar to their parents' values—they conformed to society as it was. As those born during this time came of age in the 1960s and early '70s, many more began to participate in some of what this revolution offered, moving it into the second half of the growth phase: the customization segment.

The customization segment found its highest peak during the 1970s, as the group born between 1950 and 1957 came of age. Thanks to the pioneering efforts of those who'd gone before them, this group had more choices because systems had been put in place. Everything the older kids did had now become "the way," but the younger group customized it by adding their own style. When it came time for them to rally to a cause, they chose green energy or saving animals, not just the war in Vietnam. When it was time to buy their first cars, they looked at sporty, gas-saving imports like Triumphs and MGs, and were not limited to the Mustangs and Camaros the older group loved. This group moderated many ideas from the earlier phases, bringing them into the mainstream and adding a customized twist. Evidence of their influence was apparent everywhere. People of all generations were wearing longer hair and sideburns, along with mini skirts and bell-bottom pants. The peace sign wasn't just for anti-war activists; it was becoming universal—everyone from little kids to former President Nixon adopted the cheerful greeting. Customization—that point where a product or idea reaches 50 to 90 percent of the market potential—was in full swing.

The Maturity Phase (Born After 1957)

By the time this last group came of age, the Vietnam War was over, and the stock market was rebounding from its 1974 low. This group grew up, went to work, got married, and raised their families in a society that had been radically altered by the cultural revolution. Everything was different, even the workplace. The United States had become a kinder, gentler, more integrated and inclusive society. It still wasn't perfect, but it had come a long way since the 1960s.

Regardless of whether they'd worn tie-dye in San Francisco or protested on the Washington, D.C. mall, many in the late part of this generation took the ideals of the 1960s with them for the rest of their lives. As America moved from a structured, industrial economy to the new age of information technology, this generation could still see what was possible with the tools they'd inherited from the customization segment of the growth phase. The stage was set for the next revolution.

A Generation of Continual Change

Beyond 50: A Report to the Nation on Consumers in the Marketplace (AARP, 2004) found that Americans age 45 and older are responsible for more than half of all consumer spending—and our market share is growing as our generation ages. But for every positive economic report, there are always doom-and-gloomers predicting the fall of our economy. The boomers are going to break us, they glumly announce. Social Security will fail, and the health care system will collapse.

For all their arm waving on the Sunday morning talk shows, these heralds of disaster have failed to consider not only the power and determination of the rock-and-roll generation, but also several other crucial factors. They're completely ignoring the impact of our sheer size and associated financial impact. They're disregarding the current climate of economic prosperity and our steadily increasing longevity. Perhaps most important, they're overlooking our revolutionary attitudes about traditional retirement. Each of these factors is setting the stage for the investor revolution.

For almost six decades, the rock-and-roll generation has influenced American culture and society, and our tastes have driven the American economy. As we became potential customers, it didn't take manufacturers and advertisers long to realize that the surest pathway to success was by meeting our desires. For example:

- In the late 1940s, the demand for baby food went through the roof. The late 1940s and 1950s also saw toy manufacturing become a growth industry.

- As we reached school age, we caused revolutions in school construction, teacher training, numbers of high school graduates and college attendees, and even theories of child development.

- Acne medicine and car sales boomed in the 1960s and early 1970s.

- We drove growth in housing in the late 1970s and 1980s.

- When we finally began putting money aside for the future in the mid 1980s and 1990s, financial services grew and prospered.

- In the 1990s and 2000s, sales of skin-care products, plastic surgery procedures, and all sorts of anti-aging products have boomed. We take care of ourselves with the latest in organic foods and nutritional supplements.

It's not likely that our buying power will have any less influence in the coming years.

Economic Prosperity and Changing How We Value Our Lifestyle

The Industrial Revolution created significant economic and social changes. When industrialized workers began producing everything from sprockets to scythes, the definition of success began to change. Corporate America took the reins in defining this success:

The higher you climbed the corporate ladder, the more successful you became. Wheat fields and farm life were no longer appealing when weighty business titles and polished shoes came on the scene. Young people left the farm, went to college, took jobs in cities, and began to benefit from an economic prosperity their parents had never known. They became consumers, spending their income on clothes, housing, food, goods, and services—all commodities the corporations made. Purchasing became a priority, and in a lot of ways it remains a major focus of our lives today. For most of the twentieth century, people worked hard, bought nice homes, put their children through college, and then retired to a life of leisure. But today's rock-and-rollers are beginning to want more out of life than sixty-hour workweeks that only give us the ability to buy more commodities and stockpile stuff we don't really need.

For the past year, my wife and I have hosted an Italian exchange student named Elena. In addition to being astounded by the size of everything in America—from suburban mansions and landscaped lawns to SUVs and supersize meals, she also has had questions about the pace of our lives. Her family has lived in the same modest house for generations, and she buzzes through her town's narrow streets on a scooter, like her father did as a teen. She meets her friends at a local bistro for relaxing outdoor meals, whereas I like to eat dinner on the coffee table while watching TV. She notes, "In Italy, we sit at the table as a family and discuss our day." Of course, my wife has said many times that we should do the same thing, but it sounds different coming from a 17-year-old. Needless to say, we've begun having dinner at the dining-room table, where we have great conversations. We're able to exchange ideas and compare American and Italian cultures. I've gone from inhaling my food in five minutes to relaxing and eating at a reasonable pace. Elena's questions about why we can't slow down have made me think. Do all our commodities really bring fulfillment and happiness? Why do we feel that we need these bigger houses and bigger cars in order to call ourselves successful? Most Europeans think we're nuts for having pursued this lifestyle as long as we have. The beautiful part of this realization is that I'm not the first person in my generation to understand it! As boomers, we've continued to revolutionize how we live. And part of that revolution involves changing how we think about the focused pace of work—and only work—until we retire.

One characteristic of the investor revolution is that we'll start changing the way we define *success*. Is it the sheer mass of a person's stockpiled commodities? The new definition of success includes using our wealth to create meaningful, rewarding experiences.

It takes enough people in a generation or group to change the established way of doing things. It's like the principle in physics that changing particles must achieve a critical mass. The investor revolution will change our relationship with money, but not until enough people start buying into the idea. Fortunately, the generations living in this country today are like none the world has ever seen; why should we settle for what's been the norm for decades? We have an opportunity to prosper like no other generations before us, so let's get started!

Rethinking Retirement

In the past, most people associated age 65 with retirement. But the times, they are a-changin'. Not only is the rock-and-roll generation not buying into a retirement age, they're not even buying into the traditional idea of retiring from work. *Staying Ahead of the Curve: The AARP Working in Retirement Study* (2003) indicated that half of all workers over 50 expect to work well beyond age 70.

What's driving this change? We rock-and-rollers—having grown up in an era of youth and activism—see ourselves differently in our 50s than any generation before us. We don't feel old, so why should we act it? Although we may plan to retire from our corporate jobs, we want to do something worthwhile in our free time, something that makes a difference.

Like many people in his generation, my dad spent forty years with the same employer, working at an oil refinery and counting the days until he retired. He was a hard-working man, passionate about everything he did, but he looked forward to a time of doing nothing, perhaps meeting his buddies at McDonald's for coffee, working in the yard, and watching TV. The big day finally came when he was 62 years old. He started collecting Social Security benefits, his mortgage was paid in full, and he received a nice pension—a profit-sharing plan that he rolled into his IRA. He's been able to spend his days in leisure activity; and, like many of his cohorts, he found it easy to downsize. Now that he's 78 years old, he doesn't have big ambitions and will have no problem staying financially independent for the rest of his life.

Our generation and those to follow face a different kind of future. Unlike the previous generation, we consider 62 young—too young to retire to a life of yard work and leisure. We may occasionally fantasize about leaving our jobs and spending all that extra time pursuing our favorite activities—rock climbing, playing golf, traveling, or scuba diving—but we may not be able to afford to do so in the same way the previous generation did. We don't have the same pension and profit-sharing plans the previous generation had, and who knows if Social Security will be available?

Many boomers haven't saved for retirement the way they should have. A 2006 *AARP Bulletin* poll surveyed 1,096 workers and 686 retirees age 40 and older. The poll reflected the fact that many Americans haven't realized that the baby boomer generation is facing a new reality of retirement—funding will come not from the federal government and business but from their own pockets.

In addition to the financial reasons for postponing retirement, we're also aging later, we're much more active, and we have a huge desire to remain busy and relevant until late in life. Thanks to breakthroughs in science, medicine, nutrition, and technology, most of us will enjoy good health and strength for many years to come. Today's 50-year-olds look and feel better than their parents did in their 30s. I'm convinced that I'm physically stronger and I feel better in my 50s than I did at 40, and so do many of my like-minded friends. We easily identify with baseball legend Satchel Paige, who asked, "How old would you be if you didn't know how old you were?"

Plenty of us are living a lifestyle we love, and we don't want it to end. We never want to be "over the hill." Getting old was something our grandparents did. We want to believe that if we do things right, we'll keep getting better and living profitably for decades longer than older generations imagined. We aren't willing to postpone enjoyment until we retire, and we're not sure that we're going to be happy sitting around doing nothing for 20 years. Our generation wants to build balance into our lives *now*, enjoy ourselves today, and continue that lifestyle for many years to come. Why should we wait all week to say, "Thank God it's Friday"? We want *every* day to feel as good as the weekend. When our kids are grown and our careers are at their peak, we want to approach a time in life when we have to be responsible only for ourselves. At that stage of life, our biggest concern can and should be, "How will we maintain our quality of life and make it even better?"

Take, for example, my friend Pat. Pat's hobby was flying airplanes; he was passionate about flying and spent evenings and weekends at the airport. Over the years, after earning a commercial license and an instrument rating, he decided to take his flying to the next level. He got his instructor's license and began teaching a few lessons here and there. He began to dream about retiring from his corporate job and supplementing his portfolio by teaching flying lessons when he retired.

Pat's plan worked out even better—and sooner—than he expected. Several months ago, he was given an opportunity to take early retirement at age 55. His company, like so many others, was doing a little downsizing. They offered Pat a severance package, if he wanted to use it. While other employees were moaning about layoffs and downsizing, Pat was ecstatic!

The first thing Pat did was go to the airport and talk to the management about the possibility of teaching on a more regular basis. They said, "Pat, we'd love to have you. As a matter of fact, you can do it full time if you'd like and head the flight school. We have an office upstairs, and you're welcome to it." Pat then came to me, and we reviewed his portfolio. He'd done a good job of saving over the years, and we felt that an early retirement supplemented with instructor's pay made perfectly good sense. So, Pat accepted the package and said good-bye to his former career.

Since he made the switch, Pat's car has been the first one in the airport parking lot in the morning and the last to leave at night. He's living his dreams, loving his life, and doing exactly what he wanted to do. He's even doing customer contract flying all around the Midwest. As time goes on, Pat may get burned out from teaching as many lessons as he is right now, but it will be easy for him to adapt his schedule, change his hours, and pursue his other interests.

If people like Pat are harbingers of things to come—early leaders in the revolution—transitions like his will become much more prevalent. It's likely that many of us will *not* leave our jobs, our homes, and our friends to retire to sunny communities and vegetate for two or three decades. Instead, research indicates that many of us intend to work during our "retirement" years, remaining vibrantly active and financially self-sufficient.

The old way was to go to school, work, retire, and die. I see a future with a more cyclical lifestyle: We'll work at one career for a while and then start new careers (part- or full-time) or maybe our own businesses. I see a future in which we'll run through several cycles: learn, work, adapt, take a break; and then go back to school and learn, work, and adapt again.

I see a future in which 60-somethings won't automatically retire to lives of boredom and unrewarding activities; we'll move forward from our existing positions. For many of us, semiretirement will become a viable option. Instead of the all-or-nothing approach taken by the previous generation, we may cut back our hours and spend more time doing what we love and loving what we do.

I see a future in which we'll use our knowledge, skills, and insights to become productive in exciting new ways—starting second or third careers, pursuing our calling in life, or turning a hobby into a revenue source. Maybe we'll take a sabbatical for a year or two in our 50s or early 60s to rethink our lives and rediscover our purpose. Maybe we'll go back to school and learn new skills or develop untapped passions.

I see a future in which corporations will change their models to accommodate the aging rock-and-roll generation and those who follow in our footsteps. We have a lot of skills and knowledge to offer and will for years to come. I envision corporations moving away from traditional forty-hour workweeks and letting rock-and-rollers customize their work schedules to focus on the areas they're most passionate about and in which they can add the most value. Companies that fail to adapt will see a brain drain as we leave those firms, begin our own start-up businesses, and create new cutting-edge services and ideas.

Human creativity doesn't have to end at some arbitrary age. If we're savvy, those of us who want to work will be able to choose the type and duration of our jobs not by our calendar age, but by our health, physical condition, personal disposition, desire, and a host of more important factors. We'll be able to reshape the work we do into a variety of innovative and attractive forms, including part-time work, job sharing, and new business ventures.

Many boomers see retirement as moving from structured corporate life and into their own businesses, hobby pursuits, and consulting practices. Many of these ventures will thrive, benefiting from the boomers' years of business experience and on-the-job training. As the workforce changes in America and millions of seats empty as boomers move on (and a nontraditional workforce of Generation Y is unable to follow), corporate America will find itself in the midst of a revolution, yet another led by the boomer generation. And if you don't think that's revolution enough, look for this generation to change the faces of health care, aging, and eldercare. One other revolution we'll lead? The investor revolution!

We're on the Eve of a Revolution

Until today, rock-and-rollers have been confused about the best way to manage our portfolios. We haven't been content to live with the mechanisms provided by Wall Street and its large, institutional brokerage firms. We've tried trading with traditional brokers, buying shelters and various brokerage products, and moving to discount brokerages where we traded on our own. But none of those firms recognize the dynamic—the changing—face of this generation and our needs as we age. John Havens and Paul Schervish, researchers at Boston College's Social Welfare Research Institute, predict that $41 trillion will change hands when members of the World War II and baby boom generations die. It's promoted as the most massive transfer of wealth in American history. As we move toward managing this massive transition, boomers are demanding a new investment model.

Almost all investment methods have some value. Some are better than others. Any method that's been thought out and that follows a disciplined process should work in certain market environments. The problem is that the financial environment is dynamic, which means it constantly changes. Styles go in and out of favor. Markets go from bearish to bullish and back again. And no single method or approach works in all types of environments.

Some things in life don't need to change. For instance, you don't need a super flyswatter to kill flies, and you don't need a gas-powered mousetrap to kill mice. Flies buzz and mice infest in exactly the same way they have for centuries. There is nothing dynamic about the mouse and fly environment that flyswatters and mousetraps need to adapt to, so traditional approaches still work. However, your life and financial wealth are in a totally different league. Wall Street firms don't have a process that's sufficiently dynamic for managing the investment products and tools at their disposal. They have one primary sales-driven process for selling their products. As revolutionary investors, we should demand more. As post-Napster consumers who know that technology gives us dynamic processes, and that those dynamic processes give us customized offerings, we should demand more competent, objective, client-centered advisors.

How do we know we're on the verge of an investor revolution? As is true during any movement, the early phases of a revolution have leaders and hallmark moments. Just as in the early phases of every revolution, a small percentage of innovators are taking hold of these new ideas and leading the way in the investment revolution. These innovative leaders include revolutionary portfolio managers and financial advisors who are changing our views about investing, saving, and spending. They're using a proliferation of new products and technologies to create new and better processes for adapting to dynamic environments.

As has been the case with the boomer generation from the beginning, the demand for this change hasn't come from leaders who are external academics or thinkers. It's not coming from older, wiser role models—it's coming from discerning people like you and me who are asking more from their money than their standard Wall Street brokerage firm can give. These leaders are accomplished doctors, lawyers, teachers, writers, and entrepreneurs who've begun to question what they've always been told and to use their own minds to think for themselves. They don't want to manage their money themselves, but they do want the flexibility to choose from different options. Their primary due diligence revolves around finding the right advisor who can customize their portfolios specifically for them and utilize a dynamic process to get lifelong results.

These leaders—from the rock-and-roll generation—are beginning to "retire," and instead of accepting the old, standardized market model, they're working with trusted advisors using new techniques to examine all areas of investment and customize their portfolios to meet the dynamic market environment. They're basing decisions on their unique goals and dreams. It won't be long before their way becomes the norm and the investor revolution reaches critical mass.

A Call to Action

A *potentially* exciting future doesn't automatically mean an exciting future for *everyone*. To take an active part in the excitement by shaping the future means deciding *now* how we're going to do it. Knowing this, many of us still put off planning for our later years. Why? Perhaps we've been seduced by our own youthful appearance and health; after all, we spend a lot of money and effort keeping the ravages of aging away from our bodies and brains. Of course, there's nothing wrong with appearing and feeling youthful—unless it keeps you from preparing for the future that will inevitably arrive.

Don't let that happen to you. Don't act your age—*plan* your age! By the time you finish this book, you'll be familiar with investment processes that work and ideas for maximizing your life's potential in far more creative ways. Above all, you'll have the revolutionary know-how to make a legacy of your life while you're still living it. I've always said it's more important to live a legacy than to leave one. As more and more people come to agree with me, we'll see the investor revolution take hold in monumental fashion.

You've heard the old saying: To get the same results as everyone else, do exactly what they did. If you want to age like many people of the older generation did, just follow in their footsteps—retire in your 60s, sit on the couch and watch TV or work the crossword puzzle, go to the same restaurant every week for the early-bird special, and take vacations to the same place every year. That may work for them, but if you want a different result, you'll have to do something different. Make a radical change. Join the investor revolution. Think counterintuitively.

To make your future years your best years yet, three things are required: a compelling vision of your future life, the financial freedom to pursue your interests, and a sense of health and vitality. As the Information Age reaches its maturity and we enter a new age, we're looking for the knowledge to improve our lives and the lives of those around us. It's an issue of lifestyle, really. We are the new innovators, the trailblazers, and we deserve more amenities than ever before.

Think of what we were able to accomplish as part of the cultural revolution, a bygone era when we were basically kids. We were directly responsible for setting a trend toward making America a kinder, gentler, and more inclusive society—even though we didn't have financial prowess, a functional education, or any real wisdom to speak of. What we lacked in those areas we made up for in revolutionary spirit. Now, as we approach the zenith of our lives, we have money, insight, and wisdom. We're in control, and we flip the switches that make changes occur.

Contemporary wisdom tells us that change is certain. I can say for certain that the rate of change we'll experience from here on will do nothing but gain momentum, spinning old models out of the way faster and faster. Every S-curve that follows major innovations, such as computers and the subsequent Internet, shoots to maturity at a faster rate than those before it. As revolutionary investors concerned with steering our behaviors toward an optimal life, we can either jump aboard the change train or dodge it as it passes us by.

Live Like a Revolutionary

As a generation of revolutionaries, we are again united by the common goal of changing and embracing how we live our lives and invest for our futures, altering the face of aging and retirement as we go. The information we have at our fingertips can show us the way, but it's not as easy as pointing and clicking our way to happiness. We need due diligence and motivation.

The rock-and-roll generation is entering exciting new territory where nobody has ever been. It could take us a while to pick up speed, but when we do, the sparks will fly. Not long ago, I went golfing with my longtime buddy, Steve. For whatever reason, that day we were cutting up and acting like kids on the course. Now in his early 60s, Steve is a successful businessman who's never put much credence in the idea that, as he gets older, he should become more serious. As we were joking around, Steve said his wife tells him to act his age. His stock reply is that he doesn't know how to act his age because he's never been this old before.

How should a 60-year-old boomer act? If we're supposed to act like old retirees, that's certainly not Steve. I like to think I act nothing like the prototypical 50-something of yesteryear. So how *should* we act? We should act as revolutionary as we are. We're trailblazers, and it's time we realized it. This book will show you how, as a revolutionary investor, you can supply yourself with the tools to make your future life the greatest years yet. The tide is changing, a new age is dawning. You can either be swept away, or you can wax your board and surf the wave like the wild spirit you are.

Chapter 3

Customization, Standardization, and How Money *Can* Buy Happiness

"It is not the strongest of the species that survive, nor the most intelligent, but the one most responsive to change."

—Charles Darwin, British naturalist

All this discussion of revolutions and baby boomers is great, but what does it have to do with the coming investor revolution? Why will this generation, already accustomed to change, rise up against the Wall Street status quo and demand a different way of thinking? What really needs to be done? And, most important, what can possibly be revolutionary about investing?

To answer these questions, we must return to our discussion of the S-curve, which identifies three phases that a new product goes through: innovation, growth, and maturity. Many who have studied marketing recognize some of the same categories from a standard product-adoption bell curve. Although Dent's S-curve looks a little different, it makes the same points: There are innovators, there are early adopters who contribute to the growth phase, and there are those who join the bandwagon during the maturity or last phase of the curve.

Dent suggested that it takes as long for a product to go from 10 to 50 percent of the potential market share as it does to go from 50 to 90 percent, and that when it reaches the 50 percent mark, the product makes the shift from standardized, one-size-fits-all, to customized. However, I disagree slightly with this last point: I believe that while a product is in the 50 to 90 percent buy-in range, the results are a proliferation of manufactured, standardized choices. But more choices do not translate to a customized product. At best, this situation provides only limited customization, or the ability to personalize some specific options—but the product isn't fully customized to your individual need.

It could be argued that better customization was available in the early Industrial Age, when almost everything was handmade by craftsmen. Once the transition was made to mass production of tangible products, the capacity to customize, which is a human element, was lost. It's interesting to note that, although this seems like a loss, mass production provided a huge leap ahead in many areas—a bit like taking one step back to gain two steps forward. Now we are able to come full circle.

True customization begins in the maturity phase between 90 and 100 percent buy-in, when people start asking, "Now that we have all these choices in technology or products, how do we choose what is the best fit for our need?" A revolution is a process to answer that question. When a product, industry, or age reaches the later stages of adoption, the consumer demand for a human element to help combine the overwhelming choices and information with consumers' specific needs results in true customization. This push for something different or more specific helps drive the development of new products, technologies, and processes. In other words, the maturity phase of one S-curve becomes the innovation phase of another. This overlap is where revolutions take place. New innovations revolutionize the way things were done before the technology existed.

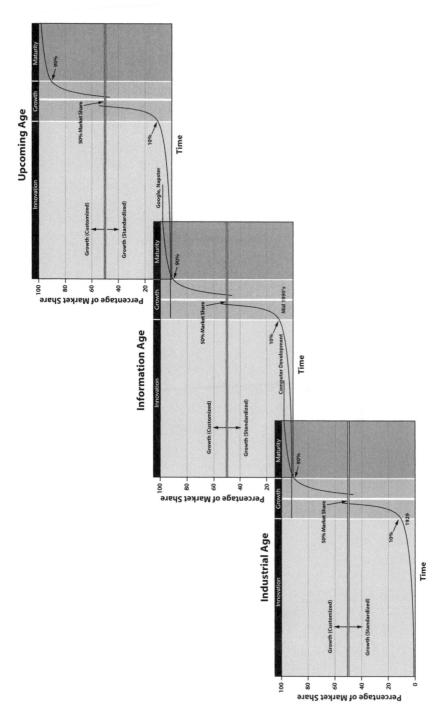

FIGURE 3.1 S-curve overlapping ages

Limited customization: The process of choosing from a set list of available mass-produced options that best meet your need.

True customization: An approach that requires a human element to execute the process of combining the available choices with the individual need to achieve a very specific result.

Looking back at our automobile example, cars were very standardized until market saturation hit about 50 percent. At that point, manufacturers started offering more choices, building cars in a variety of colors and models. However, even with all the choices available today, manufacturers still offer only limited customization. Consumers get to choose from a number of makes, models, colors, and features, but they aren't buying a custom-built car made exactly to their individual specifications and requirements. The auto industry is in the late maturity stage, having achieved limited customization of a mass-produced product. A good point to note here is that many products that are mass produced and have reached this point, like cars, will probably never become truly customized. The consumer demand or need doesn't exist.

Recently, I experienced first-hand the true customization of a mass-produced product. I asked my golf instructor to recommend a new set of irons for me. He knows my swing and me; he also knows clubs, but he doesn't sell them. As a result, I felt I could trust him to give me expert advice untainted by a conflict of interest. He said, "Because of your height, you need clubs that are one inch longer than the standard length. I would recommend three different models." He sent me to a club fitter with a list of ideas. The club fitter had a computer equipped with the latest analysis technology that measures everything from launch angle to swing speed. As I tested clubs, he asked me about the "feel" of different clubs. After the computer analysis, and given my personal preference for the feel and look of the heads, he customized clubs for me. The heads, shafts, and grips were all standardized, mass-produced products—but the fitter combined them to fit my specific needs. The club fitter utilized the latest smart technology together with his technical knowledge and good communication skills to wade through the thousands of manufactured choices and create my best choice—the one custom-ized choice that was best for me. Five years ago, I would have had to settle for standardized clubs.

Here's another example of the progression of the customization cycle: digital video recorders like TiVo. DVR technology was first tested in 1965 by major TV network CBS. TiVo-brand DVRs were launched at the 1999 Consumer Electronics Show in Las Vegas and have been a commercial success. As a mass-produced product, TiVo was developed as a result of increasing consumer demand for cus-tomized home technology options. What do DVRs do? They record television programs onto a computer drive and let you choose, man-age, and watch those programs in ways that are convenient for you. You can even record and play back a program while it's still air-ing, stopping and starting it as needed. In addition, the device has steadily developed complementary abilities, such as recording onto DVDs; skipping commercials; sharing recordings over the Internet; and using programming and remote-control facilities via PDAs, net-worked PCs, or Web browsers. Just as the automobile, in its time, led to a wave of other industries (such as road and bridge construction, gasoline/energy companies, the car dealer sales model, and so on), DVR technology is creating offshoots of industries that will further enhance and utilize the true customization model in the Information Age. The revolution is the *process of creating a customized result.*

Welcoming a Whole-Brain World

In his book *A Whole New Mind* (Riverhead, 2005), former White House speechwriter Daniel H. Pink suggests that we're on the verge of a new age. The Conceptual Age, as he calls it, will be akin to past periods of intense and invigorating change, much like the Industrial Age or even the Renaissance, which produced an unprecedented flowering of pent-up creativity. In Pink's vision of the future, we'll have an economy and a society built on the inven-tive big-picture capabilities of right-brain thinkers. We'll move from high-tech to high-concept and high-touch, which means creativity and innovation will be a boon for post-Industrial, post–Conceptual Age workers.

Pink believes, and I agree, that the Information Age is receding from center stage, just like its predecessor, the Industrial Age. However, *receding* doesn't mean *going away*. The emergence of a new age doesn't make the earlier age immediately obsolete; one age doesn't come to a sudden halt when another begins. Rather, they tend to build on each other and overlap, just as new products and technologies do. The Information Age is reaching its maturity phase while the next age is in its innovation phase. Such developments as Google, Napster, and iPods are clear examples of creative new innovations.

The new innovative stage requires a new way of thinking, but all our business models are based on an old paradigm that primarily rewarded left-brain analytical functions like conformity, linearity, and a risk-avoidance approach. The trick in the new age will be to fully integrate *both* sides of the brain. Based on what history has shown us on the continuum of the ages, there is a place for every type of thinker. As the time frame between the S-curves shrinks and society moves forward at a phenomenal rate of innovation and growth, the key will be to recognize and embrace our part in it. If you look at right- and left-brain characteristics and the rise and fall of ages, you will see that right-brain thinkers flourish more in the creative and innovative stages of a new age. The growth and standardization stages generally reward left-brain thinkers whose analytical skills develop the innovations. Later development and maturity require a better balance of whole-brain thinkers, who are best able to customize and realize the benefits of the time.

Left brain	Right brain
Logical	Random
Sequential	Intuitive
Rational	Holistic
Analytical	Synthesizing
Objective	Subjective
Looks at parts	Looks at wholes

Whole-brain thinkers bring to the real world customized, dynamic processes that were first thought up by the "What if?" right-brainers and followed by the left-brain technicians who produced the systems to convert information and choices to meet the dynamic environments. The contours of our times call for whole-brain thinkers. This new demand will also drive the consumer push for true customization in the element of human interaction. In an age where true customization is king, the right-brain requirement to match people with specific products and services to meet their individual needs will supersede the populations' complacency with standardization. Whole-brain thinkers will drive the revolution.

Great numbers of people identify more closely with the left-brain model, where such important brain functions as logical thinking and linear, rational analysis occur. That's what our parents encouraged us to embrace when our enormous baby boomer generation grew up. Among left-brain thinkers are lawyers, accountants, software engineers—the list goes on. But the future belongs to a different kind of person with a different kind of mind. The era of left-brain dominance, and the Information Age it engendered, are giving way to a new world in which right-brain qualities like inventiveness, empathy, and meaning will rise again. After all, these are the enduring qualities that adorn a fulfilled life with purpose and emotion. Where the left brain generates, the right brain resonates.

Whole-brain thinkers exist, and many of them are our best writers, consultants, and business problem-solvers. They are called free agents. I'm not talking about the highly paid athletes whose main skills are dunking a basketball or hitting a baseball—I'm referring to the fact that whole-brain thinkers are in such demand today that they can choose their own clients and projects, and work from any location they want. As technology advances, more talented individuals are choosing to work from their homes or are working part time.

Free agents exemplify the kind of revolutionary thinkers who'll play by their own rules in the next age. A big part of the next revolution relies on creativity, an inherent trait in most free agents. As the Industrial Age gained momentum, big corporations grew bigger;

they didn't want employees to be creative, because creative thinking strays from the standardized process. The bigger the corporation, the more top-down managed it became. Then, creative people began to break off and find new and better ways to deliver the product, whatever it was. They freed themselves of the old restrictive model and found that life on their terms could be even more profitable. During the innovative stage of this next age, even more new models will be created as more people buy in. The result will be a revolution. The entire model has to change in order for the revolution to take shape.

The Creaking Machinery of Standardization

As part of the maturity phase of the Information Age, where we find ourselves today, manufacturers of information technologies are able to produce their products at a very low cost. This commoditization of technologies allows new technologies to emerge at a rapid rate, which is good for us as revolutionaries. However, all these new technologies create a product overload that's difficult to wade through without knowledge and wisdom. The history of computers is a good example.

The early stages of computer development produced products that were expensive and difficult to use. In 1981, the IBM PC was introduced; over the next few years, the price of computers came down as more people became users and competition in the home personal-computer market began to heat up. Today, most families have computers in their homes, and the choices of prices and features are almost unlimited. Consumers called for and attained customization. They could order computers that were designed for home, office, or studio use and could handle graphics, music, video, or home office software. Today, for a fraction of the cost of those 1981 models, personal computers are more ubiquitous than even the early innovators imagined.

Between the endless options for computer customization and the massive, searchable databases of content, music, and video on the Internet, consumers have more choices than ever. On one hand, the industry now has the ability to produce almost unlimited alternatives to meet people's needs; on the other, the information overload and myriad possibilities have made it more difficult to find what's best for us.

Unlimited choices of customization result in information overload, which in turn coincides with the maturity phase of the S-curve. Information overload is inevitable—too much data is swirling around. Limited customization leaves us with so many alternatives that it's almost impossible to make a decision. In a classic product-push model, whoever can make the best sales pitch becomes the deciding factor in what you purchase. The decision is typically based not on how well the product suits your wants and needs, but on how skillfully you can be sold into believing you need it.

What is the answer? True customization becomes the best solution by implementing a process offered by an expert (not a salesman) to match the customer's needs. The revolution occurs when the process shifts from a product-push society (standardization) to a demand-pull society (customization)—hence society becomes the driver for the revolution, which is the process that will match choices with needs.

The old model of standardization didn't cater to us as individuals, but the new model of true customization is the driving force of entrepreneurialism. Outsourcing, as a result, is all about the progression of the standardized model. Cutting costs is critical as products become more widely available. Supply and demand dictate the Darwinian principle of survival of the fittest. Demand isn't decreasing; the delivery is just different. The new challenge is to make the delivery process an enjoyable, productive experience that gets to the one or two true customized choices that best meet the customer's needs. The more people understand the expectation of this new model, the faster the innovative stage will be driven and shaped to what benefits us most.

Standardized	Customized
Industrial Age	Information Age
Old, traditional approach	New, revolutionary approach
Commodity	Individualized
Many choices	Few true solutions
Product-push	Demand-pull
Product focused	Client focused
Static/assembly line	Dynamic process
True/false	Many truths
Right or wrong	Probability driven

Recent newspaper headlines tell us that consumers are leaning toward customization in buying everything from running shoes to coffee. Not long ago, most baristas would look at you strangely if you ordered a venti sugar-free vanilla soy latte, but today nobody bats an eye. A standard cup of Joe seems outdated and plain. Now our tastes are sophisticated and refined.

It's All in the Process

Making choices in the early stages of a product's or technology's development is simple because you don't have many choices. Early car buyers had the Model T. Early computer users had the IBM PC. In the later stages of development, too many choices lead to information overload, which often leads to anxiety. The result can be the wrong decision or no decision at all. Not making the best decision is a big reason why we have accumulated so much stuff—stuff we really don't want because it doesn't meet our individualized need.

Today, consumers are free to get the information to make choices and buy at the best prices through discount chain stores or the Internet. We can buy standardized products and services more easily and cheaply than ever, which has its ups and downs.

On the up side, the commoditization of products makes them cheap to buy, especially when information technology creates new models of distribution—we have eBay, Amazon, Travelocity, and more. However, on the down side, the ability to customize may be limited to the standardized models available, despite our access to information. Much about the Rolling Stones' famous refrain that "You can't always get what you want" rings true today. Before you can get what you want, it's important to realize what you *really* want, which means getting what you really need.

Consumers may choose to go through a process to buy a customized product or service to fit a specific need. However, the old product-push model can't deliver customization. That means consumers must sift through many choices to get to one choice—their choice. That one choice has to be the single best customized choice that meets their need. But the key is in the process. The revolution *is* the process.

The first step in coming up with a revolutionary process is answering the question, "What do I truly want?" That may not be a question you can answer. What you think you want is based on your knowledge, and if you know only the old standardized system—the sales machine—then you don't know what other choices are available. The new needs-based, client-focused, demand-pull model, as opposed to the old product-push model, requires a different behavior from the consumer. It's more important to do the due diligence to find someone who can help you define what you want.

In the second step of the revolutionary process, you enter into a creative stage to answer the question, "How do I get what I want?" This is where a trusted expert advisor comes in, whether you're buying a car or a computer, or investing. An expert advisor trained to help you understand your needs will be able to help you match what you want to the available cutting-edge choices. The consumer no longer needs to understand all the product features and choices, because the trusted advisor deals with the selection of the good or service. As consumers, our most important task is to hire the best and most competent trusted advisor possible, who will help us figure out exactly what we want and how to get it.

An example of a trusted advisor is my friend Jim Haines. As a regionally based optometrist with 26 years of experience in the field, Dr. Haines straddles a fence in two arenas. On one side, he treats patients; and on the other, he acts as a visual advisor, ensuring patients receive the right eye-care products. In optometry school in the 1970s, Haines recalls that contact lens options were limited to a standardized rigid lens. Soft lenses were just coming onto the scene, spurring a competition that eventually resulted in a proliferation of options.

"Now we have bifocal contact lenses, tinted lenses to change your eye color, lenses for certain sporting activities," Haines told me in a recent interview. "In fact, we have orange lenses that increase the contrast sensitivity of a tennis ball flying through the air, so you can recognize it a little faster than your competition. With eyeglasses, we have progressive no-line bifocals, and we have photochromic lenses that can darken in sunlight for patients. We try to customize eyewear to fit the patients' lifestyle needs. No two people are exactly the same, so we try to ask questions to find out what patients need. What do they do for their work? Do they travel a lot? Do they play a particular sport? We come up with a spectacle lens option or a contact lens to meet patients' visual demands based on those activities. We're trying to customize the delivery of eye care to the individual now. We want patients to get what the patient wants to have."

Customization and the Psychology of Money

What do standardized and customized choices have to do with investing? They've led to an information overload in investment products and information, and consumers are overwhelmed with the huge array of choices. To help them make the best choices, the investor revolution will revolve around guidance and technology. Unlike choosing a car by settling on the one pushed by the best salesperson, revolutionary investors will work with a trusted expert advisor who, like Dr. Haines, can help them understand their needs and has the technical skill to utilize a process to achieve a customized solution. People who are serious about living profitable lives need to be guided into making the right choices.

The investor revolution focuses on the process, not the nitty-gritty mechanics. Investors will find it's not as important to understand all the logistics of building an investment portfolio, for instance, as it is to understand that processes are available for managing that portfolio and the various risks involved.

Not Your Grandfather's Financial Planning

For many years, people turned to financial-planning guidance for everything from mutual funds to retirement, but the investor revolution calls for something more. Going through a financial-planning exercise is not necessarily bad; on the contrary, doing financial planning with a competent advisor can be a good and worthwhile activity. We should all take the time to plan our personal finances and implement the steps for success. But traditional financial planning isn't the best way to find out what's really important to you, and it's not dynamic enough to deal with life's many activities. Your life and finances are more dynamic than ever, and your planning and implementation process needs to be equally dynamic and flexible.

Most financial planners are trained to be left-brained technicians, and few have been trained in techniques to help clients understand what they want and set goals, and to coach clients to meet those goals. That's why they rely so heavily on written reports loaded with numbers and projections. But today's financial planning should be less about static computerized written reports and more about life—coaching investors through dynamic issues. Good coaching requires a process to help you decide what you want and then get the desired result. A good coach or advisor actively engages you in the process and helps you take ownership of the process. Then, the most important element is following the process to get the activities done to achieve the desired result.

The Importance of a Dynamic Plan

The world is dynamic. It's active, vibrant, and constantly changing, just like life. For that reason, you can craft a plan for your life, but you'll probably have to keep changing it along the way—maybe not your long-term goals, but certainly the path you take to achieve them.

That's unfortunate, because human beings like black-and-white answers. It's in our nature to lust for assurance. As much as we may love the certainty of a well-laid plan, a plan is static. As such, it stays valid only for a short time. It can't keep up with a dynamic world.

The most common mistake people make is assuming that once they have a plan, most of the work is over. In reality, the process is just beginning! Your whole life is one long planning process, ever-changing to the times and environment—and the planning process itself must be dynamic. The planning process, not the final plan, should be your main focus.

A good, dynamic financial plan should have three parts: your goals, strategies for achieving the goals, and the tasks and responsibilities for completing the strategies. The goals may not change, but the strategies should, as follows from the dynamic nature of our world. It's also important to document the plan, so you have a frame of reference for comparing and determining responsibility for the long and short term. This can be invaluable to you and others when establishing and working toward your goals and ensuring that they're followed through and fulfilled.

When a financial planner asks questions in the standardized data-collection model, the "why" is often left out. You're not likely to hear, "Why is it important to you?" When a financial planner sends out a data-collection sheet, the questions are formulated for the planner—to answer the questions she needs, not the ones you need. The *why* of the client isn't connected to the *what* of the plan. The investor's connection to the plan is shallow and diluted. This type of plan has no emotional significance to the investor.

Three Parts of a Financial Plan

A good financial plan should include:
- Your goals
- The strategies for achieving your goals
- The tasks and responsibilities for completing the strategies

---

The other problem is the separation of the right-brain process from the left brain. The financial planner primarily focuses on the left-brain function of *how to*. The right-brain questions "What is it?" and "Why do you want it?" generally aren't addressed before you look at how to get it. That approach is backward from the way it should be. You should engage in a dialogue about all these questions, not just the analytical aspects of how to execute.

Laws of the Investor Revolution

Unlike traditional financial planning, the investor revolution calls for an empowering process that allows for human nature while reducing the degree of uncertainty. Everything that goes on in life includes insecurities. That's human nature. In this day and age, the goal is to lessen the degree of uncertainty in your life and increase the comforting certainties you can count on.

Will following the process guarantee that you'll make money? You can never know that for sure. Instead of asking that question, you should be asking whether the process makes sense. Is it dynamic? What is the process's theory based on? Is it based on other theories, or is it based on laws? A process based on laws doesn't go out of favor.

The revolutionary investment process is based on the following three investment-related laws:

- *The law of supply and demand,* which states that the price of a commodity increases when the demand for that commodity exceeds the supply and decreases in the opposite case

- *The law of numbers,* which states that portfolios that drop half as much and then go up half as much as the market make a higher "risk adjusted" return.

- *The law of fluctuating markets,* which states that markets fluctuate and will continue to fluctuate, and therefore we need a number of dynamic tools and processes for dealing with the fluctuations

These laws are not style specific. They apply to all tradable markets and securities. The revolutionary process is a delivery mechanism based on these laws. The goal is to choose a trusted advisor who will follow your agreed-upon process and take advantage of the best available tools to help you get what you want.

Imagine a professional whose title is something to the effect of Information Gatherer. The IG, as we'll call this person, explores library archives, makes phone calls, digs through books, and studies references in order to compile thorough composites of information. The IG is good at his job, but not so quick in execution. One day, someone suggests that the IG might try using the Internet, which the IG has never heard of. The idea of an electronic portal to all the world's information overwhelms the IG at first. Then, the person introduces the IG to the concept of Google, a left-brained search engine. The IG realizes in a matter of seconds that he and his current information gathering process are obsolete. The Internet has revolutionized his legwork-heavy occupation, and if he doesn't adapt, he'll soon be out of business.

Google is an example of a revolutionary process that made traditional methods of getting information obsolete. The investor revolution is also about using a new process and tools that, in many ways, have made traditional Wall Street methods obsolete.

Money vs. Happiness

A central idea in the investor revolution is that we can invest ourselves and our money to become profitable individuals who aim for success in all its forms—not just financial success, but also emotional, spiritual, physical, and social successes, for instance.

Most of us make a conscious decision at an early age to take steps in our lives that will broaden our future possibilities. At age 18, we either decide to hang loose and become beach bums in Florida, or we take the initiative to refine our talents with a college education. We keep the idea of our future selves in mind as we go through dynamic phases. These decisions either limit us or open up possibilities for more opportunities when we're "futuring" an idea of what might be next in our lives.

The same can be said of which direction we'll prefer to take in the coming years. The sky, as they say, is our limit. But happiness isn't something that's easily stumbled into, and the revolution of our times lies in finding the delivery mechanism that can help bridge us between where we are today and the ideal of our optimal tomorrow. We have the power to create the possibility for things to happen, but we need the tools to steer us in the right direction when change occurs. The oncoming investor revolution will present unparalleled opportunities, and it will require the mindset of a revolutionary to realize them fully.

If you haven't been planning for that "future you" down the road—saving money to create options or exercising to keep that person fit—chances are that you won't become the ideal individual you have envisioned. Some young people exercise, and some don't, but most feel pretty good. Seven decades can change things. When I'm in Florida and see the difference between a 75-year-old who's jogging down the beach and someone about the same age whose muscles are virtually shot as he wobbles across the road, I can't help but wonder what they did or didn't do to get themselves to that point. One created the possibility to be healthy by thinking of his future self, and the other probably didn't.

To be happy in the future, you have to prepare now. As we move from the Information Age into the next age, we'll need a greater focus on relationships and experiences and a reduced focus on the accumulation of stuff. We'll need to give ourselves permission to spend money on experiences.

When we think in terms of money, we find that most stuff can be outfitted with a price tag so we know exactly what it costs. The price tag for fulfillment isn't so obvious, and it's difficult to assign a dollar amount to life experiences. That's a big mental gear-shift: The old paradigm said that money was meant to be exchanged for commodities. Paying for services was more difficult to justify, with the exception of services that improved the quality of life, such as doctors, dentists, plumbers, and repairmen. For those who come from an era of scarcity, paying for services provided by personal trainers or golf coaches may seem exorbitant or over the top. The old tradeoff used to be the idea of a vacation: a springtime jaunt to the Caribbean might cost $5,000, or you could use that money to buy a commodity you always wanted, like a down payment on a Porsche. The car would give you something tangible and useful for your money, but the vacation would come and go. So, you'd buy the Porsche. I have to admit, it's a fun car; but as with most material things, the novelty begins to wear off over time. Which buys the most units of happiness: the car or the memories of the family trip that last a lifetime? As revolutionaries, we need to ask questions like this.

This leads to an age-old idea: Money can't buy happiness. Money typically has been used to buy tangible goods and services—things you can see, hold, and show off to your friends. Happiness is a feeling you get from meaningful and rewarding experiences. As revolutionary investors, we should begin giving ourselves permission to spend money on right-brain experiences that can lead to enduring happiness. Buying tangible goods can only lead to short-lived and small increases of happiness. Once you get to the point where you're living above the worry level, more money can lead to slightly more happiness, but contentment revolves around building more rewarding experiences. If you're lying on your deathbed, and people ask you what was most important as you look back on your life, I don't think many people will muse about how excited they were to buy that new Porsche, or how buying a house with six bathrooms was the greatest thing that ever happened.

In terms of becoming profitable people, it's all about the experience. Each person has to discover what does it for them. Following the investor revolution model for happiness, a person will recall the experiences and relationships they had throughout their lives, which is where the real value is—where the emotions lie. Your personal wealth is everything you value, be it the vacations you'll never forget, the classic hot rod you're happy to customize and care for, or your most cherished relationships. If your personal wealth isn't managed properly, the result is negative experiences that have made many rich people remarkably unhappy. The investor revolution aspires to give people permission to become profitable individuals who can afford to build a fortune of experiences, balanced with the tangible things they need and want.

These days, we have so many things that storage units are popping up everywhere. We have lavished ourselves with possessions, but the quantity of what we own doesn't correlate to a greater sense of happiness. We have exchanged the possibility of experiences for possessions. How do these possessions allow us to change ourselves or the world?

Life is a checker game of choices. Too many choices, like owning too many commodities, won't necessarily make you happy. What's required to whittle away the unnecessary stuff is an entirely different delivery mechanism than what exists today. Instead of unlimited choices and unlimited information, the investor revolution will get down to specific alternatives that are exactly right for you. You'll receive the customized choice that benefits you most as a future-focused revolutionary.

As you begin to build your portfolio, doing so creates choices and options down the road. If you don't have any money, your ability to choose rewarding activities may be very limited. However, if you focus on your portfolio as well as your life, you'll achieve a good balance between personal health and financial wealth, which makes possible the experiences worth remembering.

Equally important is making the right choice in finding financial experts with the technical skill to understand your needs and structure your finances to work for you. The customized model must be delivered by trusted expert advisors who are familiar with coaching philosophies that help determine exactly what you want. However, before we continue this discussion of the new model, let's look at where we are now and why current investment management models need to be revolutionized to be successful in the future.

Chapter 4

What Do Wall Street
and Buggy Whips Have
in Common?

*"Money is to be respected; one of the worst things
you can do is handle another person's money without
respect for how hard it was to earn."*

—T. Boone Pickens, Jr.

For the sake of coming clean, I'll admit it: I'm gullible when
it comes to golf infomercials. These infomercials tend to run for
about half an hour—just the amount of time it takes to reel me into
buying the next miracle gadget for three easy payments of $39.95
plus shipping and handling. I can't resist golf training aids, whether
some sort of weighted club or a brace that locks my right elbow in
a 90-degree angle. I'm sucked in by watching the progress of guys
who start out as terrible golfers—slicing balls into the woods and
water—and then, after 10 or 15 minutes of using the product in the
infomercial, are driving perfectly straight down the middle of the
fairway.

Infomercials (or advertorials, as they're sometimes called)
always rope me into buying, mainly because I'm sold on what the
advertisers are promising. At the time, they make a lot of sense! As
you may guess, my handicap is about the same as it's always been,

even though I've accumulated a closet so full of gadgets that, last Halloween, I had enough braces and swinging devices to make a funny wacky golfer costume.

Infomercials and commercials lead us to believe that the advertiser's product is the one for us, and we'll be all the happier after we own it. I can't tell you how much happier my beard and face are as a result of my new vibrating quad razor. I don't know how I ever got a reasonable shave with only two blades! Marketers earn millions of dollars a year helping infomercial makers and direct marketers handcraft messages designed to draw people like me in effortlessly. They know that even educated people will pick up the phone if the message seems so miraculous or logical that it must be true.

Wall Street firms have also gotten in on the advertising act. We've all seen the successful-looking couple on an idyllic beach, relaxing and celebrating life. The man says to the woman that, with adjustments to her portfolio, she may be able to purchase a beach house not far from where they're sitting. The woman turns the other direction and says to her husband, "Did you hear that, honey?" The fellow you initially assumed was the husband turns out to be the devoted broker.

There are many other commercials with Wall Street brokers attending graduations, cheering for clients' kids on the soccer field, and offering heartwarming toasts at weddings. Wouldn't it be great if Wall Street firms really cared that much about us, with only our best interest in mind? The idea behind the commercials is that major Wall Street firms are so interested in becoming an integral part of the family that they'll come along for a day at the beach to discuss your future. "Far-fetched" is the only way to describe them.

In reality, Wall Street products aren't created or delivered in any such personalized fashion. These firms understand that a personalized, unbiased approach is what people want, but those of us who've been around Wall Street firms long enough know the experience is almost never like that.

The reality of dealing with your finances can sometimes seem more like a desert filled with vultures than a beach with beautiful waves and seagulls. Experiences with many brokers are superficial.

Brokerage firms can be highly impersonal, leaving you intimidated and wondering who benefits most from the investment product you just bought. The truth is, all the touchy-feely marketing illustrates the very ideal that isn't occurring. The reality is that Wall Street firms care much more about profit for themselves—more so than seeing you get that beach house.

Learning from Experience: The Wall Street Story

Making investment decisions can be a stress-inducing experience. As investors, we know mistakes can be costly. So why do most people view brokers, brokerage firms, and financial planners with such distrust? The answer lies partially in the reputation that Wall Street firms have developed throughout their history. Those famous Depression-era images of distraught investors on the ledges of Manhattan's skyscrapers hardly comfort today's prospective clients. The answer may also lie in the more recent reputation Wall Street has earned from scandals, questionable charging practices, and sullied media reports. Having been in the investment industry for 30 years, and knowing the industry from the inside, I have insight that may help pinpoint the source of distrust toward investing in traditional ways with brokerage firms.

Whether you've researched the history or read today's newspaper, it's apparent that Wall Street's current dysfunctional model is rooted as far back as Wall Street's inception. Evidence of product-pushing and commission-based processes dates back to the 1700s. In some ways, Wall Street values have evolved very little in the past three centuries. It's difficult to have missed the news in recent years about penalties levied on brokerage firms relating to the Enron, WorldCom, and Tyco scandals. It's important to understand some of the flaws of Wall Street that have existed from the beginning, in order to see how the investor revolution can swing the market's potential in your favor.

In the late 1700s, revolutionary soldiers were paid in currency called Continentals. You've probably heard the adage "not worth a Continental." Here's where it came from: In 1775, the Continental Congress authorized the limited issuance of paper currency, called Continentals, to finance the Revolutionary War. The Continental was backed by the anticipation of future tax revenues, because the Congress didn't have the authority to tax. Without a tax base and with rising inflation, the Continentals soon became worthless. In 1777, Alexander Hamilton had the idea that if the government was going to have any legitimacy, it had to make the Continental valuable. When speculators figured out that Hamilton planned to draft legislation to create taxes that would add value to the fledgling currency, they sailed for places like South Carolina and started buying Continentals. Information didn't travel quickly. It was easy for informed speculators to exploit the uninformed. Ultimately, Hamilton's legislation passed. Many of the people who were taxed had sold their Continentals to speculators for 15 cents on the dollar, and speculators, who were privy to the pending legislation, made a killing.

Most of the old stock manipulators—such as Jay Gould and Jacob Little—made a lot of money through inside information that nobody else had during the late 1800s. Back then, information traveled very slowly. Today, it's illegal to benefit from inside information, trading stocks on the open market using information gained through internal dealings or personal connections with the company. Martha Stewart learned this the hard way!

The first securities or stocks were issued in 1602 by the Dutch East India Company on the Amsterdam Stock Exchange. Financial securities were created to raise capital for corporations, municipalities, and governments. To create liquidity for those securities, investors needed an active trading market and the opportunity to trade among themselves. In the early years, speculators could sometimes manipulate the price of a stock. The result was a potential conflict of interest. Brokers encouraged people to trade so they could generate commissions; hence speculative trading was born. Wall Street was run by commissions, not investor profits.

On the heels of the Industrial Age, early Wall Street found roots in the late 1800s and was spurred on through mass speculation by the robber barons of New York City. These wealthy business magnates were perceived to have manipulated and taken advantage of the young market, creating the dawning of the age of sales-driven product pushers who made money only on the number of transactions they generated. Without transactions, they made very little money, which meant they had an incentive to persuade people to want to buy and sell all the time. Some buying and selling may have been justified, but the idea in the early days was primarily to create activity for the benefit of the firm. That was how brokers made their livings.

From the beginning, brokerage firms used a sales-, product-, and commission-based business model. Just like today, their representatives were well-trained in sales and in the basics of the many products and services offered by their firms. It's important to understand that brokerage firm representatives aren't portfolio managers or securities analysts, but are salespeople hired by the firms to sell their products. Wall Street's brokerage firms' methods have evolved little in the last couple of centuries.

Broker: An agent who charges a fee or commission for executing buy and sell orders submitted by an investor.

Portfolio manager: The person with the discretion to buy and sell securities on behalf of a client in the implementation of the client's investment strategy. The manager is generally paid a fee based on the dollar value of the assets managed.

It was advantageous for early Wall Street firms to be centered in large cities, because that's where the information and the money were. This was the era of ticker-tape. Information pertaining to live trades was fed into New York through a wire service and went to brokers and board-makers who called out specific prices and marked them on a board, sometimes creating several uproars a day. Compared to the instantaneous sharing of global information we're accustomed to today, it was a cumbersome process. One value Wall Street firms brought to the table was the research they performed, creating information for their clients. Research was generally given to the institutional clients first and then filtered down to smaller investors.

Changes in 1976 allowed Wall Street brokerage houses to charge customers negotiated commission rates. Before that, commission rates were fixed. Prior to 1976, a brokerage firm charged a client based on an industry-wide commission schedule. It wasn't long until discount brokerage firms were born. As commission rates came down, stock trading became less lucrative for brokerage firms. When commission rates were high, people tended to buy and hold. When commissions came down, it became more feasible for portfolio managers to more actively trade their accounts in an attempt to add value.

Prior to the discount brokers, brokerage firms trumpeted how good they were, never attacking other firms. The discount firms came out attacking traditional brokerage firms and their sales-based business model. Suddenly commercials for discount brokers appeared, saying, "Why pay high-priced commissions?"

Discount brokerage didn't really take off until much later than 1976, because no technical infrastructure existed to adapt to a new model. With the advent of personal computing and later the Internet, trades could be made cheaply, which led most retail brokers to avoid trading individual stocks at all and instead to focus on more profitable packaged investment products. Their packaged products were standardized, one-size-fits-all, and built to suit a wide range of investors, but they weren't nearly dynamic enough to reflect the market environment. These products included mutual funds, unit investment trusts, limited partnerships, and broker consults/investment consulting services. Although consults programs started as standardized institutional-managed programs, they were later repackaged for smaller individual accounts.

In the early 2000s, brokerage firms came under fire because of large losses of client assets in companies like Tyco, WorldCom, Enron, and many others. It was discovered that some of the brokerages had serious conflicts of interest; many Wall Street research departments refused to lower ratings on troubled stocks until it was too late.

For decades, stock research was conducted by large brokerage firms whose research departments were filled with analysts. The problem was, the brokerage firms' senior management often pressured the analysts to avoid making sell recommendations on certain companies' stocks so the firm could pursue investment banking relationships with those companies—clearly a conflict of interest. Unfortunately, many individual investors believed the research was truly independent and collectively lost billions of dollars basing their buys on the firms' recommendations. After an investigation into the large brokerages' research practices, ten large Wall Street firms admitted their culpability and paid a $1.4 billion fine in April 2003.

Salomon Smith Barney's telecom analyst, Jack Grubman, recommended Global Crossing and WorldCom stocks to his clients long after the stocks fell into a fatal decline. In 2002, Grubman was banned for life from the securities industry and fined $15 million—a minor figure for someone whose net worth is estimated to be between $50 and $70 million dollars, all gained from his Wall Street career. Grubman was a pro at analyzing stocks for the investing public while helping his firm's investment banking division, raising money for the same companies whose stocks he was recommending to clients. In the process, his Wall Street firm awarded him millions more than other analysts who may have respected the separation of research and investment banking.

Figure 4.1 shows an S-curve graph that charts the history and highlights of Wall Street as they would fall on the S-curve. It's interesting to note how this overlays the timelines of the past couple centuries that we've presented. You can easily see the impact of other historic events, such as the development of the assembly line, the Space Age, technological discoveries, and the increasing number of baby boomers, on the increased market share in Wall Street. Any industry can be charted in these terms, and the results can be both informative and enlightening.

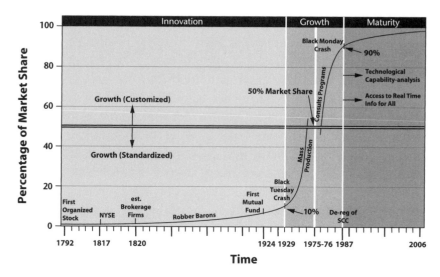

FIGURE 4.1 Wall Street S-curve

Wall Street's Short-Term Performance Pollution

I received a letter from a well-known Wall Street firm that perfectly illustrates a sales focus on short-term performance. The letter came in a hand-addressed stamped envelope. (I'm sure the firm has a postage meter, but the stamp added a personal touch.) When I opened the envelope and unfolded the letter, the personalized mood disappeared. The letterhead was photocopied. There was no name, date, or address, just a generic message touting a stock-picking process and three years of performance. The broker claimed to have the solution to all my financial issues—obviously without knowing what they were. His product would meet my needs regardless of what my needs were. He hoped that I would call and transfer my account immediately.

Why would the firm send such a letter? This mass-produced and impersonal approach is like shooting a gun in the air and hoping a duck flies by. The letter is a throwback to the old mass-mail techniques of the 1980s. Not only was it cold, but this particular firm saw fit to make the letter's initiator a first vice president and senior financial advisor. I wondered if his firm's management or his coworkers—or even the legal department—would be appalled if they saw this letter. Nowhere in the letter was there a disclaimer telling me past performance isn't a guarantee of future results. The material shouldn't have passed the firm's compliance review. Although mass sales approaches like this are becoming rarer at major firms, they reflect the culture and values shared by many Wall Street firms. It seems that only the threat of scandal has been sufficient to create some changes in this culture.

Typical Wall Street standardized sales approaches neglect to focus on each client's true potential as an investor. The aim is to have Joe Investor open the letter, see great performance over the last three years, and then call the firm with enthusiastic requests to come aboard. The same letter was probably sent blindly to hundreds of other potential investors. It's like a personal trainer advising the same workout to every client who walks in the gym. If a personal trainer approached her job that way, you'd see elderly people straining on bench-press machines and beefcake musclemen trying yoga poses. The standardized workout doesn't suit everybody. It would be a dangerous system, and attending that gym would be a serious dice-roll in terms of each client's health.

Letters or other mass-market techniques—including expensive television ad campaigns—illustrate a generic process designed to capture prospective clients with promises of short-term performance and close client-advisor relationships. Wall Street's investing process is a standardized, mass-produced attempt to lure in clients who buy into short-term performance sales pollution.

Even with the best personal trainer, who focuses exclusively on one client at a time, it's not certain that each client will slim down to 8 percent body fat and become a tennis star. Nobody can tell you exactly what your potential is, but following a process to get into the best physical condition possible will invariably make you healthier. The process has to make sense for you—and that process can't include a regimen of potato chips and couch naps if you really want to be fit. Simply watching a belly-buster infomercial won't do you much good either, because you have to take action. No process is fail-safe, but the right process will produce a greater result than homogenous, standardized strategies—both in the gym and in the investment world.

You can't control the market, but you can control your process for investing. You need a process that makes sense to you—one that utilizes the basic principles we'll visit in later chapters. If the process doesn't resonate or doesn't utilize the innovative tools that are now at your disposal, you should look elsewhere. Locked into the old one-size-fits-all model, Wall Street investment products have grown to be synonymous with homogeny.

With the standardized investment product model, everybody looks the same. You've probably never seen your real portfolio manager—the person who makes the decisions about security selection—let alone hung out with him or her at the beach. With the investor revolution, consumers are demanding customization in ways that should soon make the old models seem obsolete, especially when it comes to handling your money. With good coaching from a trusted advisor, you'll find inherent communication lines and customization that Wall Street doesn't have time to deliver.

Playing the Name Game

A few weeks ago, I was enjoying a pleasant Saturday on the local golf course when I ran into an old friend of mine, Joe, a Wall Street financial consultant. We talked a while about our golf scores, our families, the weather, and finally the direction of our careers. Joe's eyes fired up when he pulled his newly redesigned business card from his wallet. Just below his name, the words Wealth Manager were embellished in an important-looking font. I had to scratch my head a little.

"Now I can tell people what I do," said Joe. "I do wealth management."

Further into our conversation, it became clear that Joe isn't doing anything too differently than he has for the last 30 years. He's respected in his firm and is good at what he does, but he's doing the same things he's always done. Our conversation left me a little puzzled. I suspect Joe felt his previous Stockbroker and Financial Consultant titles were beginning to lose their luster; so, like countless others who abide by the old Wall Street model, he's searching for a fresh spin on his old ways.

I agree that financial advisors should evolve and improve their skills. Unfortunately, more effort has gone into polishing image and redefining titles than improving methods. With a few buzzwords in their vocabulary and a little doctoring of their business cards, many brokers today are changing their stories to make their services seem like the new thing, when little has changed from what they were doing years ago. As my editor says, "It's like putting fresh lipstick on the same old pig!"

Despite Wall Street's many outdated approaches, investors have had a few good runs. Unfortunately, those runs had much more to do with luck or a bull market than with skill. If you resemble the vast majority of investors, your luck eventually ran out when the bull market ended. You could see your successes were marked by short periods of unusual market swings. You gave back any gains, and possibly more, and were left wondering what happened. Old investment approaches and beliefs don't die easily, especially when they continue to be promoted by a Wall Street sales system designed to sell products and generate profits for "the firm"—many times at investors' expense. There are financial advisors who try to do the right thing for their clients, but the Wall Street commission-based business model doesn't support client-centered advice.

Wall Street has a tendency to create trendy titles for its salespeople and then change the titles when times are tough. In the early days of Wall Street, men who sold securities started out as "a customer's man," which gave way to the more familiar title of "stockbroker." All of a sudden, the Stockbroker title became unpopular, so these salespeople morphed themselves into financial consultants. After a few years, the Financial Consultant title became passé, so next there were financial planners—and, in accordance with the trend, we've seen the emergence of wealth managers. Especially in the '80s, if the title of Financial Planner or Tax Shelter Specialist developed a questionable reputation, the title was soon discarded for another, and so on. As my golfer pal demonstrated, the trend continues today, creating new campaigns for the same old-model platform. Salespeople still generally do the same things they've always done. Nothing has changed but the title.

The Issue of Core Competency

The problem with the sales-driven approach is that the emphasis is on selling standardized products and not on delivering service that custom-fits your investments to your needs. In finance, there are lots of options and areas to choose from, and plenty of brokers and consultants to present them to you. But do these individuals possess the core technical competency, or the essential level of expertise, to personalize anything that's best for you? Or is their objective primarily to get you to buy?

The answer is most often the latter, because the investment "experts" following the outdated model lack the core competency to tailor a plan that's best for individual investors. Webster's Dictionary of English defines core competency as "a defined level of expertise that is essential or fundamental to a particular job." Doctors, lawyers, and architects are examples of specialists who exhibit their expertise on a daily basis—and if they're inefficient in execution, the results are immediate and potentially tragic.

Today brokerage firms prefer to have brokers focus their energies on selling standardized packaged products like mutual funds, annuities, and consults programs. Training revolves around product knowledge and few, if any, investment-management techniques. Wall Street firms liked the idea of creating a fee-based model to supplement the commissions generated from brokerage products. However, whether the benefit justifies a fee is questionable.

Consults program: An investment program in which a consultant structures a portfolio, generally using outside money managers/brokers.

Most Wall Street advisors, consultants, or brokers—regardless of the title—are first and foremost salespeople, not portfolio managers, and they don't provide the kind of service that has traditionally justified a management fee. Without the kind of experience that justifies a management fee, how could the firms switch from commission to a fee-based model? The answer was to charge an all-inclusive or wrap fee in lieu of transaction commissions. Part of the wrap fee was used to pay portfolio managers to manage the portfolios. As a result, investment management consulting was born.

Investment management consultants are generally associated with brokerage firms or are financial planners. They combine several style-specific portfolio managers or several mutual funds of varying styles for each of their clients. They have limited if any interaction and contact with these style-specific managers. Over time, the consultant switches managers to maintain an optimal blend of different styles. As you'll learn in the next chapter, such an approach has quite a few problems.

Some brokerage firms have created a guided portfolio-management programs for their advisors. Such programs generally recommend stocks for the advisors to select for their clients. The firm also has diversification requirements for the portfolios. The training and experience required for these programs vary from firm to firm, ranging from a short seminar and test to extensive training and testing. For the most part, the brokerage firms' portfolio-management programs are viable options for investors. They do create a structured investment process. One of the biggest benefits is the more functional relationship that is created between advisor and client. That said, the experience and credentials of most of these broker/managers aren't as extensive as you see with most independent portfolio-management firms. But in the course of all these products and all this training, one thing is lost: the client. Rarely is your financial advisor or wealth manager trained to help coach you so you can connect your money to your life goals.

My preferred approach is a fee-based philosophy that adheres to the idea that a financial advisor is paid a fee based on the amount of assets in the entire portfolio. The advisor isn't compensated by commissions generated from the buying and selling of securities; rather, the fee is based on the total value of the assets the advisor manages, thereby eliminating the inborn conflict of interest in a sales approach. The more money the advisor is able to make for you, the more the advisor is compensated. Additionally, I believe it's critically important for your advisor to work closely with you to set goals based on your life—and to have you work with a coach if needed to stay on track. Suffice it to say, the fee-based model has a higher probability of keeping the clients' best interest in mind. It achieves a win-win result that creates an incentive for the advisor to focus more on money-management skills and less on selling. It's important for investors who've been locked into the old model to realize that the investor revolution presents a choice—and the ability for investors to take a step in a new direction.

Learning from Old Mistakes

Many of our parents or grandparents were burned by the stock market crash of 1929. During the crash, if you had a balanced portfolio that contained both stocks and bonds, and if you had paid cash for the securities (not borrowing on margin), you saw a dramatic drop in your stocks but saw your bonds go up, helping stabilize your portfolio's decline. The Depression also caused a huge disinflationary environment, which means prices of most goods and services dropped precipitously. Something that cost $100 in 1928 cost $75.66 in 1933, during the Depression. The real effect of the market crash on purchasing power wouldn't have been as dramatic as it was, if all this were taken into account.

Let's contrast that with the '70s. When we saw the market drop during that time, we also saw high inflation. As a result, prices went higher. That same $100 item from 1928 would have cost $332 in 1976. Coupled with high inflation, the stock market fall was a calamity. Because of these bad experiences, stocks weren't a popular investment with our parents and grandparents. They were understandably driven by scarcity and fear.

When I got started in the investment business in 1977, the trading volume on the New York Stock Exchange (NYSE) was about 14 million shares per day. I considered 20 million shares to be a big day. (Today, generally more than 500 million shares a day are traded.) Stocks weren't popular, and the systems for managing stock portfolios weren't sophisticated. One of the best options people had for creating a diversified portfolio was to buy mutual funds. Most mutual funds were bought through a broker and had substantial front-end loads, or sales expenses. That sales expense was sometimes as much as 7 percent of the initial investment. Many insurance agents and independent brokers sold funds with even higher sales commissions.

As mutual funds became more popular, some mutual fund companies like Vanguard began to offer no-load funds, which were devoid of sales commissions. That didn't mean there weren't any fees; the fund obviously had management fees, operations fees, and costs for trading securities. However, the internal fees were taken directly from the funds, and investors didn't see the expenses deducted from their accounts. Because they weren't privy to the day-to-day growth of the market, it was easy for investors to lose track of what these no-load funds cost, because the investors only saw returns.

Taking Hold of the New Possibility

A few years ago (on April Fool's Day), I left the portfolio-management division of a major brokerage firm and that side of the industry for good. There was no significance to my leaving on April 1; it was just that I'd seen enough of the old model and its shortcomings. Similar to changes in the banking industry, brokerage firms had undergone consolidations and were becoming larger, more standardized, and more hierarchical in management. I didn't see anything dynamic coming from the brokerage industry. In my 30 years in the business, I'd gone from the nervous kid making cold calls to someone with the experience to know a better method could exist—to know that a customized model was needed. I'd worked with firms of all sizes and specialties, from one of the smallest (a five-branch firm on Wall Street) to the biggest financial mega-house in existence. During my career, I fulfilled every capacity from a stockbroker to a financial planner to an investment management consultant to, ultimately, a portfolio manager. I saw the culture from the inside and went through all the training the Wall Street conglomerates could offer.

Looking back, I'm grateful for every iota of my experience. But I knew times had changed. I could see the revolution coming. The time and technology are right for creating a new model to revolutionize investors' experience in dealing with their money.

Buggy Whips

What do Wall Street and buggy whips have in common? The buggy whip, as we all know, was made obsolete near the turn of the twentieth century by the advent of automobiles; suddenly nobody needed a device to crack a horse into motion. By drawing the parallel between Wall Street and buggy whips, I'm not suggesting that Wall Street is obsolete—quite the contrary. Wall Street has had its own revolution in the development of new investment products and faster, more efficient, inexpensive ways to execute transactions.

The old Wall Street sales-based delivery model—the process—is what is obsolete. Today there are many investment choices, many market environments, and many investors' needs. The investor revolution is about creating a new process to match investments to the ever-changing market environment and thereby meet individuals' personal needs. Wall Street firms are entrenched and locked into their old product sales model. I personally don't believe they will be able to adjust and embrace a new process.

Industries go into the customization phase kicking and screaming. Nobody wants to move from standardized to customized products; it's too big of a logistical hassle. As industries develop and consumers' tastes become more specific, however, customization represents a natural progression, a different kind of business model delivering a more refined service. Wall Street is too invested in its old ways to customize itself to a degree revolutionary investors would—or should—be happy with.

In the grand scheme of things, investment management is still very much in the early stages of development. Never before has the wealth existed to invigorate it. In 1977, a $100,000 account represented a sizeable client portfolio. These days, portfolios are much larger, which shows the popularity financial services has gained in spite of its sometimes questionable reputation. There are more investors now, and, accordingly, the existing assets are much larger. A new approach to overseeing those assets is called for in these revolutionary times, and portfolios aren't set in motion these days with the crack of a buggy whip or any similarly defunct tool.

Tradition, as Woody Allen once said, is the illusion of permanence—the idea that what's always been will always be. To become a revolutionary investor, you need to buck the traditional confines of Wall Street investment practices to find what's best for you. You have the freedom to abandon old strategies for what will benefit you most, to pursue innovations in your life that will lead to a more profitable tomorrow, and to move toward a new solution. Today's investors are independent enough to take advantage of changes as they arise, and that sounds pretty revolutionary to me.

Chapter 5

How Does This
Affect Me?

*"You did what you knew how to do, and when you
knew better, you did better."*

—Maya Angelou, poet and educator

Regardless of whom you've worked with in the past, you know
that market movements change and mutate over time. Investment
strategies once considered conservative may now seem aggressive,
and vice versa. It may seem ironic that, as a revolutionary investor,
your best bet when it comes to investing is to stick to a discipline
with well-thought-out rules. It's important to have a dynamic rules-
based investment process that adapts to different market environments and proves that sticking to the game plan, in all actuality, is
the best game plan. It's up to each individual investor, however, to
discover which plan is right for them.

My goal as a portfolio manager and educator is to inspire confidence in investors by teaching them to focus on the process and the
achievement of lifelong results. You already know that short-term
performance, as pushed by Wall Street firms, is more about sales than
achieving lifelong results. The markets and portfolio-management
strategies are ever changing, and thus no single investment style
works in all market environments.

I was having lunch with a client, a woman who was passionate about charitable giving. In the past, she had a bad experience
with the standardized investment approaches typical of Wall Street.

She was used to living on an emotional rollercoaster, watching the market swing up and down, and worrying that she wouldn't have enough money for her expenses, let alone her giving. After lunch, we reviewed her portfolio. During the prior quarter the market had fallen about 7 percent. Her portfolio was down about 4 percent. Free from fear and focused on the long term, she looked at the dip in the market and simply said, "It's just a fluctuation."

I knew how significant a step that was for her because of her previous experience. With some financial education, she knew that her portfolio-management parameters were being followed. The peace of mind that could only come from understanding her investment process gave her the confidence to continue to make a difference in the world through her giving. Now she can focus on living her purpose and passion, confident that her customized portfolio will serve her well in the long run.

Today we focus on the most efficient investment *process*. It's a way of adhering to a disciplined approach. The key to leading a prosperous life in every sense is finding the right approach that works for you, one that's custom-built with your vision of an optimal tomorrow in mind. With the myriad of "investment professionals" out there and the old practices of Wall Street still highly commercialized, finding the right approach can seem like the modern version of the needle in the haystack. Taking ownership of your financial decisions is up to you, but as you begin to understand and embrace the investor revolution, you may find the time is right to explore options beyond the traditional Wall Street methods.

Financial Planning: A Step in the Right Direction

One day in 1979, my monthly copy of *Registered Representative* magazine arrived in the mail. The cover showed a man in a business suit, his open shirt revealing a Superman-type outfit with the letters CFP® emblazoned across the chest. Inside, an article described a brand-new kind of advisor: a Certified Financial Planner™. This highly trained professional helps clients tackle their most important issues—areas like estate planning, insurance needs, retirement goals, investment planning, and more. Intrigued, I became a CFP and changed jobs to work for a major Wall Street firm as a regional financial planning director, handling financial planning for some of the firm's clients with the highest net worth—for a very high fee. The process was exhaustive for both parties. It was mostly a left-brain activity with lots of numbers and projections. The financial plan was more than 200 pages long. The counseling was good, but the process was much more about the reports and investment products than about coaching and getting ongoing results. As a few years passed, I learned that although financial planning has many benefits, it doesn't always achieve its intended results. The model contains three inherent flaws:

1. *Most financial planners give investment advice, but very few have investment credentials.* This means that few of them have professional designations in security analysis or portfolio management. Although there are some excellent planners who provide high-quality service, most focus on gathering financial data and producing a one-time, written plan containing future projections.

2. *The fee structure tends to put more emphasis on the plan and less on the counseling.* Planners generally charge a flat fee, a fee based on net worth, or an hourly fee. In most cases, planners put more emphasis on the planning process and less on financial coaching, client education, or counseling; this is partly due to the one-time, fee-for-plan business model. Some planners are fee- and commission-based, a model that causes them to focus more on implementing the part of the plan that requires buying products and less on non-commission-generating activities. Once the plan is done, there's no incentive to help you to stick to it.

3. *Financial planners typically refer portfolio-management duties to an investment-management firm or mutual fund.* The planner often charges a quarterly fee to "manage the managers," which means the client ends

up paying layers of fees—often to other divisions of the same large company. In many cases, the planner doesn't have the expertise or specialized designations to justify the additional costs. With rare exceptions, the referred investment-management firm or fund manager isn't apprised of the client's personal objectives, tax concerns, or financial plan, resulting in a lack of coordination between the plan and the actual investment management.

Financial planner: A generalist who helps individuals and corporations meet their long-term financial objectives by analyzing the client's status and setting a program to achieve those goals.

Certified Financial Planner™ (CFP®): A financial advisor who takes extensive exams in the areas of financial planning, taxes, insurance, estate planning, and retirement and also completes continuing education programs each year to maintain certification status.

Furthermore, any financial advisor can call himself or herself a financial planner. Two certifications are available: Certified Financial Planner and Chartered Financial Consultant. The former is the more rigorous program. However, there are no parameters guiding the requirements to provide certain services or charge certain fees.

One client, Jim, described an experience that illustrates some of the drawbacks inherent in financial planning. When Jim's wife decided to accept an early retirement offer, the couple had some decisions to make about the severance package she received. They consulted a financial planner who recommended that they invest in mutual funds.

Jim described the process this way: "Basically, it forced us to gather all our information in one location, and it forced us to look at our income, expenses, and tax liabilities, but that was something we could have done on our own. We never saw it as any kind of strategy. There was no real direction about what we should do to maximize income or minimize taxes. We had several accounts in several different places, but there was never any coordinated review of all our assets. It was more of an organizational tool for information gathering.

"With the financial planners," Jim continued, "we really didn't have any education. They picked certain mutual funds, but I had to ask for information about the stocks that the mutual funds invested in. They would have been perfectly comfortable just telling me what mutual funds they were going to invest in, and then I was supposed to sit back and watch what happened."

As Jim discovered, a typical financial planner attempts to predict whether you'll reach your investment objectives at a certain age, based on projected rates of return and inflation. "Of course, none of those things panned out," Jim observed, "because the rate of return didn't follow their projections, and there was no follow-up."

What Jim didn't get was any sort of meaningful counseling on how to create a plan based on his and his wife's life goals. They didn't strategically match their plan to where they wanted to be, and without that connection, they didn't stay on track. The planner was constrained by a business model—a one-time, fee-for-plan with no counseling on anything to do with Jim's life—which was more to blame for the planner's lack of follow-up than the planner's skills. Jim's poor investment results were also partly due to the fact that the planner wasn't a portfolio manager.

Investors with serious money—those with good savings plans or good retirement packages and those who have been smart about growing their nest eggs—have tried financial planning and ended up with nicely bound plans that were only partially implemented and, in many ways due to our dynamic lives, were obsolete shortly after delivery. Or they dealt with salespeople whose primary objective was to sell them more products. Jim and his wife even tried managing their investments themselves through discount brokerages that cost less but lacked the extensive high-level advice required by individuals with high net worth.

Chartered Financial Consultant (ChFC): A financial professional who has completed a course which includes the courses for CFP certification and builds on that knowledge with classes in estate, retirement, and in-depth financial planning applications. Certification requires three years of full-time business experience and continuing education.

The Magic Number Myth

A lot of people sit down with financial planners and hear about a number. This number is supposed to be the amount of money you need to retire on and be secure in your future. The financial planners work through a complicated formula to help you figure out your own number based on income, age, and when you want to retire, but they fail to take into account the fact that retirement looks different for everyone. No one number works for any and all investors.

Some years ago, a couple I know—Ken and Janet—walked into an office with a sign above the door that promoted the professionals inside as brokers and financial planners. Ken and Janet sat down to speak with a financial planner who immediately asked what their objective was. The couple, who were both successful professionals, had always been the types to plan, and they said they'd like to retire in 10 years.

"That's interesting," said the planner. "How much money do you spend now?"

The couple replied that their typical spending was around $10,000 a month. The planner used this information to begin calculating the amount of assets Ken and Janet would need to accumulate before they could retire. Then, the planner started running through projections, figuring in how many assets Ken and Janet had already accumulated, which tax bracket they were in, the inflation rate, and numerous other variables, until he came up with a solid figure. The planner's approach involved many calculations, numbers, and projections.

"The bottom line," said the planner, "is you're going to have to save $5,000 a month in addition to your existing portfolio to be able to retire in 10 years."

Ken and Janet took the advice and followed it for a while, tucking away exactly $5,000 each month. That figure started to cause some discomfort, so gradually they strayed from saving exactly that much. Eventually, they stopped saving all together and became frustrated.

They began to look elsewhere for advice, eventually contacting a personal wealth coach to help counsel them through the process. "We want to retire in 10 years," said Ken to the personal wealth coach, "and we were told we have to save $5,000 a month to get there. It's binding us financially, and we can't motivate ourselves to do it any longer."

The personal wealth coach asked the frustrated couple, "What does retirement look like to you?" They thought about it and replied that retirement involved lying in a lounge chair on the beach, listening to crashing waves. Not discounting the couple's retirement vision, the personal wealth coach asked if that was what they wanted to do for the rest of their lives. They said no. The coach asked if perhaps they should focus on their passions, which could lead to even greater fulfillment.

Personal wealth coach: A financial professional who helps people envision, monitor, and achieve maximum fulfillment from both their tangible and intangible wealth. The coach accomplishes these important goals by focusing on two key components: financial/investment services and personal life issues.

Ken responded that his passion was woodworking. Janet was interested in buying and selling antiques. Before long, they began the process of figuring out how Ken and Janet could do more than retire; they drafted a plan that allowed them the financial capability to graduate from their professional lives into work that involved their true passions—in this case, a small woodworking shop built onto their home and consignment space in a local antiques shop. They worked through the process based on their vision of what would follow their working lives and left the experience with a far more alluring outlook on their future than endless months of tucking money away.

Ken and Janet were urged not to focus on building a retirement nest egg, but to think of ways in which their passions might become a profitable goal to aim toward. The techniques and approaches of a personal wealth coach usually leave clients surprised with themselves and not frustrated by their impending circumstances.

Most investors are curious to know the exact number it will take so that they can consider themselves financially independent. Later in this book, as we begin to investigate probabilities of returns, you'll learn that the number question is extremely difficult to answer. As we revolutionary boomers begin to consider retirement, we find that we're dealing with a different time than our parents experienced; their income was predictable, and they were more likely to bank their livelihoods on pension funds, profit-sharing plans, and Social Security. They were also more likely to retire to leisure and live a shorter life. Finding their number was a much easier process, but for us there are so many different variables that it's hard to define an exact number that will financially cushion us as we age. In the case of Ken and Janet, their financial planner saw their options as saving money and growing it by investing. The financial planner never looked at other potential sources of income in addition to their investment portfolio. A financial planner couldn't look toward the future to see Ken's love of woodworking translating to a small shop where he repairs and refinishes antiques that Janet resells in her profitable antiques business.

Investment Management Consultants: Not Quite Right Either

You've now begun to understand the need for a creative or revolutionary model and to see that many traditional approaches may not be the best solution to help you reach your future goals.

As you explore your options, you'll most likely encounter investment management consultants. These advisors combine several style-specific investment managers or mutual funds of certain styles for each of their clients. Consultants have limited interaction and contact with these style-specific investment managers, and over time, they switch style-specific managers to maintain what they hope is an optimal blend of different styles. Investment management consulting puts the financial advisor in more of a counseling role after the process has begun. The investment management consultant may be able to give objective advice and protect the investor from the psychological risk of circumventing the process.

Investment management consultant: A financial advisor who typically structures a client's portfolio using outside money managers/brokers or mutual funds. Such a person is sometimes called a "manager of the managers" or the manager of a broker consults program.

Stockbroker or broker: An agent (typically a registered representative of a NYSE firm) who charges a commission for executing buy and sell orders submitted by an investor. A broker is prohibited from charging a fee for advice while trading.

There are some benefits to combining different investment management styles and managers. However, investment management consulting isn't without its flaws. These simple bullet points are a good summary of investment management consultant flaws you should keep in mind:

- *Few investment management consultants have ever acted as portfolio managers,* so they're making recommendations about a discipline they've never practiced. Their process generally isn't dynamic enough to adjust standardized managers to market conditions. They also don't address changing market volatility over time.

- *They typically base their recommendations on past performance* and correlation among the managers over too short of a period. Unfortunately, today's best-performing style-specific managers are often the worst-performing managers in the future (because their specific styles go in and out of favor). It takes many years to generate risk and performance data that has any meaningful statistical significance.

- *They choose style-specific institutional money managers who tend to carry many stocks.* The result: The client ends up with hundreds (or, in the case of mutual funds, thousands) of individual stock positions. Because the money managers don't communicate with each other, the client gets cross-ownership (for example, three different managers buying IBM) and uncoordinated changes in asset allocation and weighting.

- *They put a great deal of emphasis on measuring the various managers against market indices.* Most of their reporting is on a quarterly basis. Measuring performance over short-term periods, as anywhere from one quarter to a few years, has no statistical significance and creates a great deal of emotional or psychological risk for the client/ investor, which may be the biggest risk of all.

- *Because the money managers own so many stocks, their stock-picking ability is watered down.* Their performance tends to be highly correlated with the style or index they use as a benchmark (such as large-cap growth, mid-cap value, contrarian, and so on).

- *When a consultant changes investment managers, it's usually due to underperformance,* which normally results less from the manager's decision-making process than his style going out of favor. Many times, by the time the manager is changed, the style comes back into favor.

- *Hiring and firing style-specific managers can be expensive.* Liquidating your entire portfolio and buying new securities from a new manager can lead to significant tax consequences and shifts in allocation. When you add all the transaction costs, the impact costs of trades in the market, the consultant's fee, and the manager's fee, you can see why it becomes difficult to receive financial value. Often an investment management consultant's program can cost twice what it would cost to utilize a portfolio manager.

> **Certified Investment Management Consultant (CIMC):** An investment professional who has completed extensive course work and passed NASD-proctored examinations for Levels I and II of the Institute for Certified Investment Management Consultants' course. The CIMC must also meet requirements related to experience in consulting and managed accounts, adhere to a code of ethics, and meet continuing education requirements.
>
> **Style-specific investment manager:** A manager who invests in just one style of investments, such as growth stocks, value stocks, contrarian stocks, and so on, or mutual funds with a very specific investment focus.

As a result of these considerations, investment management consulting isn't the best model available.

Portfolio Management: A Better Approach

Now we come to yet another category of investment advising—portfolio management. What makes it different than the other approaches? Institutional portfolio-management firms manage money in a standardized, style-specific manner. Often, investment-management consultants hire institutional portfolio managers to manage their clients' portfolios. Institutional portfolio managers rarely communicate directly with their clients and generally don't customize portfolios to meet the client's individual objectives. Given that revolutionary investors want to meet their specific goals and that customization is now possible, what if we took the concept of portfolio management one step further? What if we found a revolutionary portfolio manager?

Institutional portfolio manager: The person with the discretion to buy and sell securities on behalf of a client in the implementation of the client's investment strategy. The manager is generally paid a fee based on the dollar value of the assets managed.

Revolutionary portfolio manager: A financial professional who plays an educational and consultative role, teaching clients about the fundamentals of investing, customizing and managing the portfolio based on the clients' specific objectives and risk parameters, and counseling them through difficult periods in the market.

The first step we'd take is to use a fee-based portfolio-management system. This business model encourages portfolio managers to educate clients and take a customized approach. The fee-based system, unlike the commission-based model, dramatically reduces the potential for conflicts of interest. However, in a traditional Wall Street investment firm, this fee-based system can be a problem. The fee structure is sometimes prohibitively high because of all the layers that needed to be paid—the investment firm itself, the portfolio manager, the brokers, and the mutual fund companies and managers. That leads us to step two.

The second step in creating a process that reflects what today's investor really needs is working in an environment flexible and small enough to provide expert advice but also keep fees at a reasonable level. Combined with an element of coaching so both the portfolio manager and client understand the strategy, we have the basic elements of the investor revolution process. As with any revolution, this one will come from dissatisfaction with the current regime among the masses.

Two keys distinguish a revolutionary portfolio manager: discretionary authority to select securities for clients and a personal relationship with clients. If you have a financial advisor who recommends a product or service that is managed by someone other than herself, she is product-centered, or a distributor of standardized investment products. (Keep in mind that some portfolio managers use specific index funds within their portfolios as risk-management tools; that isn't the same thing as selecting other managers to choose funds for the portfolio.) On the other hand, an advisor who makes the investment decisions on a discretionary basis is a portfolio manager. On a fee-only basis, portfolio managers don't benefit from individual transactions. A broker—the person making the trades directed by the portfolio manager—receives a commission on the transactions. This separates the person making investment decisions from the person selling investment products.

Traditionally, institutional portfolio management has taken a hands-off approach when it comes to client interaction. For the most part, these people are securities analysts who manage portfolios in a standardized way, and rarely is a client relationship ever established. This results in an inability for these managers to coach their clients through difficult periods in the market, which can create significant psychological risk.

Investors who are leading the revolution will work with independent, regionally-based portfolio managers who focus more on high-net-worth individuals and smaller- to medium-sized companies. Most cities have several independent portfolio-management firms offering regionally-based management and a personalized touch. At these firms, you meet the people who are making the decisions that relate to your money and who thereby become familiar with you and your investment goals. These firms have a process for managing portfolios using a rules-based system.

Some portfolio managers are obviously better than others. To be able to justify an expense for their services, portfolio managers must show that they have a process to add reasonable value over and above what investing in an index fund would do. These managers have different styles, but if they have the credentials and experience we'll discuss in the next section, as well as an investment discipline they can articulate, and you are able to make a personal connection with them, then they should be worth considering for managing your portfolio.

What Is a Portfolio Manager?

It's important to make an informed decision when selecting a portfolio manager. As you begin to pay attention to roles, titles, and credentials, it's imperative that you know and can speak directly to the person who manages your portfolio so he can customize it to your specific needs.

Independent portfolio managers generally have training or designations in fundamental and/or technical analysis and modern portfolio theory. The two top designations for portfolio managers are Chartered Market Technician (CMT) and Chartered Financial Analyst® (CFA®). Both designations require at least three years of study and testing. Both certifications also carry requirements for work experience. As confusing as they may seem, the right acronyms are invaluable finds when it comes to picking the portfolio manager who's best for your money. Portfolio-management firms sometimes have their own in-house programs to teach their portfolio managers the fundamentals of portfolio management.

Although credentials don't necessarily guarantee you're getting a great portfolio manager, they provide a starting point and show that the portfolio manager has gone through training, taken a certification exam, and focused on investment analysis for a certain period. Anyone can call herself a portfolio manager; you must look deeper to make sure you're getting what you want. Portfolio-management experience and process are most important.

Following are a few of the financial areas I feel investors should keep in mind when researching portfolio managers. To be successful at managing portfolios, a manager needs to be skilled in five disciplines:

1. *Fundamentals of portfolio management and construction of efficient portfolios:* The most efficient portfolio is the one with the highest return and least risk. Rational investors want the highest return possible within their personal risk-comfort range.

2. *Stock and bond selection:* The manager must have a clear understanding of the psychology of markets. Technical market analysis is based on the irrefutable law of supply and demand. Supply and demand causes stocks and markets to go up and down. The law of supply and demand is the result of changes in human behavior, which are somewhat predictable.

3. *Volatility management:* The manager must utilize a method to measure and identify the changing volatility in markets, securities, and portfolios, and then use a process to make adjustments in the asset allocation and securities based on that. The key to obtaining the highest risk-adjusted return is to maintain a consistent level of volatility in the portfolio.

4. *Investor education:* The manager must possess an understanding of and have the ability to communicate common myths and psychological stumbling blocks that cause individual investors to make wrong decisions. Client coaching is crucial to helping investors avoid one of the biggest risks in investing: psychological risk. Psychological risk causes people to abandon their investment discipline during difficult times and to be too optimistic at the top of the market and too pessimistic at the bottom of the market.

5. *Investment Policy Statement (IPS):* The manager must establish written investment objectives and make every attempt to follow an investment process that quantifies and encompasses the investment objectives of the investor. An IPS should also address quality-of-life issues involving the role and purpose of money for the investor.

Manage Your Own Portfolio, or Seek the Help of a Professional?

You may have begun to realize that managing a substantial portfolio is a complex and time-consuming endeavor. You have just begun to scratch the surface of the knowledge you need to have lifelong success at investing. So, the question arises: Should you try to manage your own portfolio or let a trained professional do it for you? Like Jim in our earlier example, you may be looking for the answer to that question but may not know who can answer it for you.

You may think I have only one answer because I make a living in the field of investment management. But in reality, I can't answer this question for you. Before you make the first phone call or surf the first Web site, you should ask yourself what you really want.

There's no right or wrong answer. Your answer depends on your personal style: Are you a hands-on type who likes to personally oversee every aspect of your life? Are you fascinated with the financial markets? Do you consider portfolio management an enjoyable and productive activity or hobby? If so, then you'll probably be willing to manage your portfolio on your own.

On the other hand, do you consider the management of investments a burden? Do you want to understand the nuances of investing but not necessarily handle the day-to-day maintenance? Are you comfortable delegating important tasks to others? If so, you may want to consider working with a portfolio manager.

Which Financial Advisor Option Is Right for You?

Questions to ask yourself:
- Do I want to manage my own portfolio?
- What am I looking for—assistance with buying/selling securities, investment advice, or both?
- How do I want to pay a financial advisor? Fees? Commissions?

- How important is it that my financial advisor have a fiduciary responsibility to put my interests first?

Questions to ask a potential advisor:

- Do you manage portfolios on a discretionary basis?
- Are you compensated by management fees, commissions, or both?
- Do you recommend or utilize mutual funds or outside money managers or products?
- Are you compensated by commissions on trades?
- What are your credentials?
- Can you articulate your investment process in a way that I can understand?
- How much experience do you have?

Locating the Right Portfolio Manager

Trust is a huge factor in investment management. It goes without saying that you need to trust the person in charge of your assets. When trust is established, often through a personal connection with the portfolio manager, the investor typically experiences peace of mind regarding how her money is being handled. The real task on the investor's part is to perform the due diligence to find the right portfolio manager, which is more important than understanding all the complexities of the products currently available in the market. Here are some keys to locating the right portfolio manager:

1. *It's impossible to get a customized result if you don't know the portfolio manager.* A customized investment program is more than just the portfolio itself. It should include individualized investor education, coaching through investment objectives, and the creation of an Investment Policy Statement, which connects the client's specific objectives to the investment process. Ongoing counseling is important to protect the investor from the psychological risk of circumventing the investment process.

2. *There is no substitute for experience.* Be sure your
    portfolio manager has been around long enough to have
    experienced many different market environments. In 2000,
    many portfolio managers with the best short-term track
    records had never experienced a bear market. They didn't
    recognize the need to practice risk management. A a result,
    they lost billions of investor dollars as well as, in many
    cases, their jobs.

3. *Make sure you generally understand the portfolio
    manager's investment process and that you're comfortable
    with it.* The manager should discuss things like his buy
    and sell discipline, how he defines and manages various
    kinds of risk, the kinds of securities he considers, and how
    he diversifies his portfolios. Does he manage the portfolio
    with consideration given to tax implications? You should
    jointly define expectations for communication. You may
    require quarterly meetings or may want to meet on an as-
    needed basis.

4. *Portfolio management is primarily a left-brain (analytical)
    activity.* Find out if the portfolio-management firm
    offers some right-brain services that are included in the
    management fee, such as financial planning, personal
    wealth management, or coaching.

One benefit of the Information Age coupled with the growing wealth of individual investors is that there are more and more
regionally-based portfolio management firms. Most of these firms
specialize in working with investors with minimum assets generally
ranging from around $500,000 to $1,000,000. You can find these
firms by asking for referrals from friends or doing an Internet search
for investment-management firms coupled with the name of your
closest major city. Looking at a portfolio-management firm's Web
site is a great way to gather information and to get a first impression
prior to narrowing your choices for firms to interview.

Most portfolio managers like to meet with potential clients several times to be sure of a fit. There is rarely a charge for the introductory process. You should feel comfortable bringing your statements with you for the manager to analyze. Expect discussions about what you want and your investment experiences— both good and bad. The portfolio manager will probably want to provide you with some investment education, which is important to help get you and the manager speaking the same language for better communication.

You should be able to sever your relationship at any time with no penalties. For that reason, it's as important to the manager as it is to you that everyone feels at ease. The last thing the manager wants is for you to change your mind after a year or two. The manager has a lot of time and effort invested in setting up your accounts and creating your portfolio. You should fully expect and feel comfortable with the idea of having a long-term relationship with your portfolio-management firm. If you have any second thoughts, then you should probably keep looking.

When I met Larry and Lindsay, a couple in their 50s, they had already met with several potential financial advisors, none of whom had presented a logical investment strategy they felt fit them. By the time I met them, they were loaded with questions.

We talked about what they wanted in an advisory relationship and the types of clients with whom I'd successfully worked in the past. After a series of meetings over the next few weeks, we decided to work together. As an added benefit, we've also become good friends.

Larry and Lindsay used an intelligent approach to finding an investment advisor. "You have to educate yourself," Larry suggested. "You have to know what you're going after, and the only way to do that is to talk with people, find out what their philosophy is, and find out if you agree with that philosophy. We discounted certain people right away because their personalities didn't mesh with ours."

Lean Toward a Fee-Based System

Although there is no perfect way for an advisor to charge for services, some methods are better than others. A fee-only portfolio manager is more likely to give objective advice than someone who's commission-based. Portfolio managers have the discretion to trade securities in your portfolio; they should not be compensated by commissions, because they're then paid for trading. Fee-only portfolio managers make more money when the portfolio goes up and less when it goes down, and they get their management fee only as long as they're managing the portfolio. Therefore it's important for them to keep the client happy. Their fee-based system presents more of a win-win dynamic—the advisor can earn more only if the value of the portfolio increases, which is also a win for the investor. It's a better incentive system.

Working with a portfolio-management firm is entirely different than working with a brokerage firm. Keep in mind that as of July 2005, the SEC requires that brokerage firms offering fee-based advice make this disclosure (verbatim):

"Your account is a brokerage account and not an advisory account. Our interests may not always be the same as yours. Please ask us questions to make sure you understand your rights and our obligations to you, including the extent of our obligations to disclose conflicts of interest and to act in your best interest. We are paid both by you and, sometimes, by people who compensate us based on what you buy. Therefore, our profits and our salespersons' compensation may vary by product and over time."

In a study commissioned by TD Ameritrade in 2006, of 1,000 U.S. investors, 79 percent of respondents said they would be less likely to go to a brokerage firm for financial advice after reading the disclosure. However, 43 percent were unaware that brokers and independent portfolio managers are held to different standards by the SEC—and that of the two, only independent portfolio managers are required to act in the best interests of their client in all aspects of their relationship, and only independent portfolio managers are required to disclose all conflicts of interest. It's not always easy to find advice you can trust.

Securities and Exchange Commission (SEC): The agency charged with administering federal securities laws in the U.S. The SEC oversees the key participants in the securities world, including securities exchanges, securities brokers and dealers, investment advisors, and mutual funds. The SEC is concerned primarily with promoting the disclosure of important market-related information, maintaining fair dealing, and protecting against fraud.

Customizing the Investment Industry

The investment industry isn't alone in its gravitation toward client-centered, customized approaches. Retailers latched on to this idea some time ago, and many have found it to reap lucrative results and more satisfied customers. Drugstore giant Walgreens is a prime example. In the 1960s, Walgreens' patrons could expect to find a diner and soda fountain in most locations, along with the standard pharmacy products. Back then, the retailer was more focused on maximizing its profit margin per store, not per customer. In time, Walgreens' executives learned that in order for their good company to become a great company, adjustments were needed, which in effect would change their entire business model. So, Walgreens began to axe its expenses. The diners and soda fountains were done away with to help pay for amenities like drive-up windows and photography studios. The sacrifice was the loss of a sheer volume of customers, but the gain came in persuading each pharmacy customer to spend more by offering more. Walgreens changed its model to be more client-focused and, in effect, blew much of its competition from the 1960s out of the water.

Harry Dent, Jr., the S-curve specialist from earlier chapters, noticed a trend in the early 1990s that showed successful companies moving from standardized retail products to value discount goods and finally to customized premium products. In *The Great Boom Ahead* (Hyperion, 1993), Dent noted how the future economy would "provide enough growth markets for both emerging and maturing companies that can appeal to the growing quality and customized segments of the marketplace." Dent whittled down the three basic market segments in all industries, and labeled companies with one of the following three classifications: yellow-chip, red-chip, or blue-chip.

Yellow-chip: "…The old standard-quality, mass-market sector in the economy. These shrinking companies in mature industries grew up in the assembly-line standardized economy."

Red-chip: "This is the value/discount segment…have made substantial incremental improvements over standard-quality yellow firms, bringing high value into their industries with discount prices, often accompanied by improved quality and service…"

Blue-chip: "The blue-chip is the premium sector of an industry, specializing in high quality, customization, and personalized service with fast response and quick delivery."
(From *The Great Boom Ahead*, Harry S. Dent, Jr. [Hyperion, 1993].)

The yellow-chip companies of Dent's economic outlook were the old, standard-quality companies, or the mass-market sector of a particular industry. In the early 1990s, according to Dent, these included household names like Sears in the retail business, Pizza Hut in food delivery, Ford and GM in the automobile industry, and Merrill Lynch in the investment world.

Next were the red-chip companies, or the value/discount segment, which Dent called "a hotspot in the past, but only warm in the future." Included in this group were maturing retail giants like Wal-Mart, clothiers such as Levis, and, in the investment world, Wall Street discount brokers like Charles Schwab. Dent noticed the trend of red-chip companies making "substantial incremental improvements over standard-quality yellow firms, bringing generally standardized value into their industries with discount prices and improved quality and service." However streamlined the approach of red-chip companies may have seemed, there was still much ground between them and the superior blue-chip sector.

Blue-chip companies represent the premium sector of all industries. Dent's blue-chip term denotes the highest-quality companies, which specialize in customization and personal high-tech service with fast response and quick delivery. Representing this echelon, according to Dent, were automobile manufacturers such as BMW and Lexus, clothiers like Giorgio Armani, delivery services like Federal Express, and, in the investment world, local financial firms. "The future in the coming boom," wrote Dent, "will belong to the companies that fit my definition of blue-chip." Advancements in technology and access to information will allow highly mobile creative firms to revolutionize business models and overtake the giants of the past.

Similar to the successful companies in each economy that tended to focus more on the individual, the ultimate evolution of the investment industry will be to adjust the standard commission-based model to a more personalized fee-based approach. The fee-based model promotes more objectivity and client-centered treatment, representing the blue-chip processes of investing. The number-one incentive for advocates of the fee-based model is to keep clients content with the direction of their portfolio, because the more the portfolio swings in a positive direction, the greater the compensation for the portfolio manager. The fee-based approach tends to eliminate the conflict of interest that's inherent in the sales-based model and thereby ensures that all decisions made within the portfolio are being made in the client's best interest. Customized portfolio management coupled with personal wealth coaching, or personal wealth management, is the investment industry's answer to the need for a blue-chip investment company.

Personal wealth management: A unique process for helping people achieve and manage total wealth and abundance in all forms. It can be broken down into two critical areas: personal wealth coaching and customized portfolio management.

Looking at the Big Picture

Revolutionary portfolio managers need to be good educators who are able to teach revolutionary concepts and explain them in a way that resonates with clients. Investing is counterintuitive: You always feel good at the top and dismal at the bottom. The true risk that investors primarily deal with lies within themselves. Individuals have done more than their fair share of blowing themselves up financially, and it's not always Wall Street's fault. Time and time again, investors have dumped hundreds of thousands of dollars into investments that they haven't begun to understand, which shows an extreme lack of diligence on their part. Time and time again, those steps have resulted in sharp losses, which signal that investors need to better inform themselves about who's right for the job of handling their money.

Not only do investors need to select the right financial advisor, but they need to be sure to use the right tools. One tool is the Investment Policy Statement, which helps investors adhere to more rational objectives. Developed with a portfolio manager, the IPS outlines and prescribes a prudent and acceptable investment philosophy while defining the investment-management procedures and long-term goals for the investor. Creating an IPS compels investors to put their investment strategy in writing and commit to a disciplined investment plan. An IPS is like a blueprint and a report card combined, and it's just one example of a tool that revolutionary investors are utilizing in crafting their futures.

A written IPS helps an investor maintain a long-term focus when short-term market events create distress and perhaps cause you to question your policy. With the objective, predetermined plan outlined in the IPS, an investor avoids emotional decision-making and concentrates on rules-based decision-making. Basically, you become a more disciplined investor. The outcome is a more predictable investment strategy focused on consistency and long-term results.

To realize your potential as a revolutionary investor, you need not only a dynamic investment-management process, but also the right-brain processes that can help add color to your financial objectives. Personal wealth management represents a new approach in the way we invest in our lives. The investor revolution will help us get there.

Funny as it may sound, investing can be an exhilarating and interesting experience. Are investors afraid to change? Of course. Do they want to be safe? Sure. But there are ways to be safe that can also add value. Anyone can cash out and go bury their money in the backyard. Sure, when it's buried, the money is somewhat safe and is always where you put it. If you're going to bury your money, however, why not move it to a savings account, another option for safekeeping? In a savings account, your money may actually make you more money, kicking back about 4 percent interest per year. That's a better deal, but is it the best you can do?

If you want to do better than that, you need to select the best investment process for you. Throughout my professional experience, I know I added value for my clients as a broker, a financial planner, an investment-management consultant, and a portfolio manager. I have many friends who are highly competent advisors, and they too add value for their clients. However, many of today's investors are looking for something more. That "something more" is a revolutionary portfolio manager who practices personal wealth management and is paid a fee to maximize the investor's entire portfolio and structure it in a way that best suits the investor's specific life and goals.

Aaron is a 56-year-old physician. When he became responsible for managing his family's $18 million fortune, he sought guidance from a tax attorney and a broker. "My lawyer emphasized estate tax planning," he recalled. "He set up two charitable remainder unit trusts and a charitable lead trust. With a family limited partnership—another idea of the tax lawyer's—I found myself making choices so that the avoidance of estate taxes seemed to make my life worse instead of better. The broker showed a personal interest in me but not in any way toward furthering my goals or helping me use the money to have a better life. The money seemed like the only goal. He'd say, 'Buy bonds' but never made any suggestions about balancing my total portfolio."

Aaron knew he wanted a comprehensive approach to coordinating his life issues with his personal finances. He also wanted a fee-based service, free from conflicts of interest. Working with a personal wealth manager has met those needs.

Challenge yourself to join the revolution! Challenge yourself to move to the next level, beyond standardized solutions for complex issues, and to work with an advisor who integrates your future life vision and goals with personal wealth coaching and portfolio management customized to meet your changing needs. What revolutionary investors are looking for can only be found in personal wealth management—the blue-chip answer to an evolving environment. Individual investors must decide what's best for them. Making an informed choice is the first step in producing the best results for the future.

Chapter 6

Personal Wealth Management: Getting Your Life Involved in Your Money

"The best way to predict the future is to invent it."

—Alan Kay

If, like most people, you watch commercials during baseball, basketball, or football games, you probably think wealth management has something to do with investing or financial planning. That's how the term is used these days. It's been made a generic catchall with no true definition, used by virtually everyone in the financial industry to sell investment products, financial planning, life insurance, and more. You see it printed on business cards, embroidered on polo shirts, and hanging over office entryways.

Wealth management should not be confused with *personal wealth management*. When you think of your *personal* wealth, what comes to mind? Your personal wealth includes more than just money and tangibles. It includes your relationships, your health, your compelling vision of the future—everything that means something to you and makes your life what it is.

The personal wealth management approach can be broken down into two critical areas: personal wealth coaching and customized portfolio management. The revolutionary process of personal wealth management keeps the investor in mind at all times. It utilizes a number of innovative tools designed exclusively to help investors develop the personalized strategies just right for them, and to monitor, review, and update those strategies to meet dynamic circumstances. In some cases, a portfolio manager is trained as a personal wealth coach. In other firms, the two roles are held by two different people.

Personal wealth coaching: No matter who you are or what you do, your future life will include a number of transitions, and each one will affect your personal finances. That's why the personal wealth management philosophy combines personal life issues with financial and investment-management services and coaching. A personal wealth coach helps people envision, monitor, and achieve maximum fulfillment from both their tangible and intangible wealth. Good coaches do more than advise; they draw out the best from you and work with you to create a higher level of abundance than you ever could have imagined. Successful personal wealth coaching relies on using visioning techniques to connect personal goals with money.

Customized portfolio management: Because no one investment portfolio is appropriate for all investors, a portfolio should be customized with attention to the investor's clearly defined goals and objectives. For many years, customized service was reserved only for major institutional investors and the world's wealthiest families, who assembled teams of professional advisors to coordinate all aspects of their personal finances and portfolio management. With the personal wealth management approach, the portfolio manager knows the investors personally and is committed to helping them achieve total wealth and abundance. The portfolio manager should play an educational and consultative role, teaching investors about the fundamentals of investing, customizing and managing the portfolio based on their specific needs and risk parameters, and counseling them through difficult periods in the market.

Some advisors tell you what to do—remember the old commercial, "When EF Hutton talks, people listen"? Unlike a traditional advisor, a coach guides you through the process of discovering what *you* want and need and how to best achieve it. Great coaches help you improve your expertise in the affairs of your own life and elicit your commitment to achieving your goals. In short, they help you achieve your ultimate performance and constantly improve your personal best. The personal wealth coach has to know you and be vested in you, and has to have great people skills to figure out exactly what you want.

This chapter will focus on personal wealth coaching, and chapters 7 and 8 will cover customized portfolio management. When both components of personal wealth management are combined—when each discipline overlaps correctly—the end result is the investor's peace of mind and a profitable investment portfolio.

Coaching and the Psychology of Money

Personal wealth coaching includes the process of self-inquiry and self-evaluation. It also offers an additional process: the discovery of how intangible assets can be invested in a future vision. The personal wealth coach focuses on two key components: financial/investment services and personal life issues.

In addressing the first component, financial/investment service, a personal wealth coach begins by helping investors address their relationship with money. In talking with investors, coaches rarely hear anyone say, "I want to make the most money I can possibly make; I want nothing more than great riches." On the contrary, most people express the following concerns about their relationship with money:

- *Financial concerns when they step away from their careers.* They've grown accustomed to being the family breadwinners, and then they suddenly move on and settle for living on their portfolio's returns. Retirement may sound relaxing, but these investors often feel disempowered, as if they've worked their whole lives only to start over again. They have shifted from earning money and accumulating it to living from their portfolio.

- *Feelings of guilt* in relation to their high net worth, which signifies a flaw in their functional relationship with wealth. Psychologically, their wealth has become, for one reason or another, a troubling burden.

- *Worry about how their money will affect their children or their ultimate heirs.* For example, they fear their children or heirs will never have the same appreciation for money as they do, because their appreciation came from building the wealth themselves.

- *Fears about money* (especially for women) when they aren't involved in the decision-making process or don't understand it. Many women worry that they will become widowed and will have to make decisions about their money that they aren't comfortable making because they lack knowledge or expertise.

- *Anxiety or uncomfortable feelings* about dealing with money—often the result of a divorce or the death of a spouse.

Thinking about a career transition always brings to mind the story of a longtime friend, Dwight, a psychiatrist in his mid-80s who had stepped down from his day-to-day office hours a few years before we met. Interestingly, Dwight still practiced from time to time, seeing clients a few hours a week. I asked Dwight one day why he continued to work, because I knew he'd saved more than enough to be financially independent during his post-career years. I suspected that Dwight was passionate about the psychiatrist role he'd known all his life and didn't feel he could let go of it.

"Well, that's part of it," Dwight said. "I like what I do. But really, it's something as simple as this: I like to make money. It's just something I like to do."

By continuing to earn an income, Dwight got the feeling that his skills were still valuable. He didn't need the money, but he liked the idea that he could still bring it in. It added a degree of value to Dwight's life and, as simple as it may sound, it made him feel good about himself.

We all want to feel that our talents and careers generate a value that is uniquely our own. The ability to choose is a central function to the entire personal wealth coaching process. Regardless of his financial independence, Dwight was never encouraged to leave his practice and retire; rather, he molded his practice around his life. He graduated from his full-time career to his passion, an activity that made his life rich in a valuable way.

People like Dwight who make the shift from a full-time career may have questions like:

- How much can I spend?

- How do I get the money I need? Do I take it from my portfolio?

- How much money do I need to leave in my portfolio?

- Do I need to change my investment objectives?

These are all questions that a personal wealth coach will help the investor answer.

Too often, we're consumed by our daily activities and the progression of our careers, and we forget what an absolute joy it was to make money in the first place. It's easy to become emotionally detached from our earnings. When those earnings are deposited electronically, settled into an account by computers, and then distributed electronically to pay off debts like water bills and car payments, it's hard to feel we've accomplished something by making money. The money is in, out, and gone before we see it. The old idea of a paycheck and a pat on the back for a job well done has virtually disappeared, and sometimes that connection is sorely missed.

As kids, many people learn this direct and tangible connection to money. They earn money (by babysitting or mowing lawns), and then they spend it. Whether they blow it all on milkshakes or CDs (personally, I blew mine on baseball cards), they have the ability to choose. They can take part in a larger economy, no matter the scale. We forget this fundamental connection as we age—or, rather, we forget that it's still there. We take it for granted as it becomes part of who we are, until one day it jumps out at us (or our personal wealth coach points it out).

A couple of years ago, I found myself speaking in front of a local group at a small public library in southern Indiana. Exactly six people showed up. I spoke for a while and then entertained questions. All six attendees bought one of my books, and everyone paid in cash and handed the bills directly to me. I suddenly realized something I hadn't experienced in a long time—a direct connection to my money. This $150 in cash I was holding was suddenly much more important to me than any amount of money sitting in a bank.

While my wife and I enjoyed a great meal on the way home, I told her how the experience at the library was different than managing money. At the library, I talked about what really interests me and then left with actual dollars in my pocket, earnings I accumulated because people were directly appreciative of my work. When we left the restaurant, I paid the bill in cash, not with the usual credit card. I was amazed at this connection between the money I'd earned and the dinner we'd enjoyed. It was easier to make the connection between my work and pay. The experience that night seemed more gratifying and personal, and I almost felt like the sweaty kid who was handed a few dollars for a job well done.

One of the goals of personal wealth coaching is to help people deal with the different feelings associated with money. Not all of those feelings are negative, as you've seen. Earning money can give you the feeling that your services are valued, and it's important that the connection between that service and the subsequent value be continually reiterated. That feeling gets lost in the perpetual scurry of chasing paychecks you barely see. A personal wealth coach can help you recover and sustain positive feelings about money.

The Wealth Management Benchmark®— A New Coaching Tool

A crucial task in the area of financial/investment services is to help investors prioritize and manage their personal wealth. There is a significant difference between what you would do with a traditional financial planner and what you do with a personal wealth coach. Both will produce a financial planning document—although the type and length of the document will be dramatically different—but the personal wealth coach will help walk you through the plan. The personal wealth coach will ensure that you review important present and future concerns. Then, he will work with you to take the necessary steps to meet your goals and make sure you've done everything possible to plan for the future.

Managing your personal wealth is similar to managing an investment. Just like the dynamic and ever-changing financial markets, your life and financial issues are dynamic and ever changing. Keeping up with this change requires many tools and a process for selecting the right tool at the right time. One process for managing your personal wealth is the Wealth Management Benchmark (WMB).

The WMB is an ongoing process that evolved from financial planning. Unlike traditional financial planning, it applies to *all* areas of personal wealth and is administered by a personal wealth coach. The goal is to ensure that all areas of your personal wealth are addressed.

If you've ever worked with large Wall Street firms' financial planners, they may have charged you a lot of money for a traditional financial planning report. The "best" ones come in a fancy binder with your name stamped in gold—and can be over 200 pages long. But these reports are often an exercise in futility, because financial planners and clients rarely implement many of the plan's recommendations. Be honest: The binder probably ended up collecting dust on a shelf somewhere beside an unread copy of *Moby Dick*, right?

The inherent downside of financial planning is that it's generally more about creating the report than it is about execution and coaching. The WMB is a tool that changes the dull left-brain process to a more creative whole-brain experience. It turns financial planning into a coaching process: Investors take ownership of the process, and the coach helps them figure out what they want and how to achieve it instead of telling them what the coach thinks they should do.

The process begins by addressing specific issues in six personal wealth management categories: Net Worth and Cash Management,

Investment Planning, Retirement Planning, Estate and Legacy Planning, Life Planning, and Asset and Income Protection. For each issue, the investor is asked to do three things:

1. Determine the issue's importance.

2. Determine the issue's completeness.

3. Determine a time frame for completion.

For example, one area addressed in the WMB is, "Confirm that all tax-advantaged employee benefits are being maximized." Is doing that important to you? Do you think it would be a good idea to spend some time looking at your 401(k) plan, deferred compensation plan, or other benefits to ensure that you have taken appropriate advantage of those opportunities? If so, you go onto the next question.

Next, what's your level of completeness in confirming that you're maximizing all employee benefits? Let's say you've thought about it a little, but you haven't gone as far as you'd like. In that case, you need to go to step three to determine the time frame for completion. Let's say you'd be willing to do it within the next six months. Then you appropriately select that answer. You similarly move through the other issues on the worksheet. (An abbreviated version of the WMB is included in the appendix so you can try it yourself.)

After completing the WMB checklist, participants receive a personal Wealth Management Benchmark report—an easy-to-read scale that lets them measure their progress against the goals they've set for themselves. Working with their personal wealth coach, they decide which areas, if any, require immediate professional assistance, determine an optimum schedule for reviewing and evaluating their progress, and establish the best ways to continue fine-tuning their individualized personal wealth management strategy.

The WMB approach is superior in many respects to traditional financial planning. Financial planning (as obvious as this may sound) involves finances and the planning of finances—it's primarily a left-brain activity that requires gathering your financial data and jumping into a bland process steeped in numbers and projections. As anyone who's been through it can tell you, it's not much fun, and it has little (if anything) to do with your life issues and what's important to you. Today, most of the plan comes out of a computer and takes the form of projections and numbers. In truth, the process is more about the fancy final report and less about getting results. It's an inaccurate way to present your life in a dynamic world.

People often worry that they've left something undone. Maybe their wills aren't up to date, or their investments have too much risk or aren't in balance. The world is unpredictable—emergencies arise, markets go down, accidents happen. With the WMB, it's unlikely that anything will occur that hasn't been addressed. This revolutionary new tool helps individuals avoid unforced errors—those unseen obstacles that can derail a financial train but are easily prevented with a little advance planning. The WMB provides the peace of mind that comes from knowing no stone has been left unturned and no question has been left unanswered.

Please note that it's not important for a personal wealth coach to be an expert in every category of the Wealth Management Benchmark. For example, when the WMB says, "Discuss your estate and legacy philosophy with an estate planning advisor," the personal wealth manager's job is to get you in touch with a professional who can address this issue. Another example is the periodic physicals most investors require, another checklist item on the WMB. It's important to keep that physical on the perennial list—if that's what the investor wants—so that the investor will schedule an appointment with a physician. Personal wealth management is about helping investors define what's important to them and then encouraging them to execute those decisions.

The WMB offers a glimpse of who you really are and where you want to go—places a dusty financial plan could never take you. The WMB empowers you and puts you in charge. It's the umbrella over all aspects of personal wealth management, but it's only one of many revolutionary facets in this new approach.

Staying on Track with a Personal Wealth Coach

Earlier in this chapter, you learned that personal wealth coaching covers two key areas: financial/investment services and personal life issues. Whereas the financial/investment services component is addressed with the Wealth Management Benchmark, the second key is staying on track with personal life issues. A personal wealth coach can help you create a compelling vision of your future life, discover a vision of possibilities, and outline the goals to achieve it.

Coaching is typically a sports term for the guidance given to help individuals or teams improve and win. It became a familiar term in the business world in the 1980s when Thomas Leonard, a key player in the field of business, used it for the guidance he gave executives to be the best at the game of business. Now coaching is a growing industry, especially in light of highly visible coaches. One of the most well-known, introduced by Oprah Winfrey to TV audiences, is Dr. Phil McGraw, who gained notoriety with his famous saying, "How is that working for you?"

Today, there are coaches for just about everything you can think of—career coaches, life coaches, vision coaches, personal trainers, and more. Personal wealth coaches differ from all these in that a personal wealth coach focuses on the connection of investors and their money. Where can you find a personal wealth coach to advise you on your personal wealth issues? Few investment firms have one on staff, but some advisors have taken training in personal wealth coaching or have an alliance with a personal wealth coach. One popular program in personal wealth coaching is the Vision Coach Relationship Builder™, created by Steve Moeller, founder of American Business Visions.

The role of the personal wealth coach is to be a catalyst of change, to help this new generation of investors who are demanding the revolution, those who seek to create profitable lives for themselves and others. A personal wealth coach must be someone who is skilled at integrating all aspects of personal wealth—from health to relationships to goals—and connecting those with your money.

Personal wealth coaching can help people discover how living purposefully improves longevity and the quality of life.

Coaching During Times of Change

A personal wealth coach can be especially important during worrisome times of transition and change, such as retiring from a career, surviving the loss of a spouse, receiving an inheritance, moving from a familiar residence, going back to school, taking time for a sabbatical, or dealing with a divorce.

As people face aging and life changes, it's natural to ask, "What do I want next?" For some, "next" might be the next meal, the next job, the next marital partner, or the next stage of life, such as retirement. Whatever "next" may be, most of the time you're making decisions intended to create peace of mind in your future.

When you're going through change and figuring out what's next, you need a good balance of optimism and realism. In this age of overwhelming options, a coach is valuable and necessary, because the process of constructing tomorrows isn't as automatic as it was for previous generations. Our Depression-era parents and grandparents had their futures automatically mapped out: Go to school, get a job, raise a family, and then retire, ideally with a pension supported by a Social Security check. Our lives aren't so simple.

Let's contrast our grandparents with us. A friend describes memories of sitting on the back porch talking with his grandfather at his country home. His grandfather would wave as the neighbors drove by, not worrying too much about his future, concerned only with tending his garden the following day. His grandfather was only 64! Now contrast that image with former Beatle Paul McCartney, who just turned 64 and has no intention of rocking on a porch; he's too busy rocking on stage!

What's your idea of what will make you feel fulfilled in your future? Be careful that your dream isn't too automatic. Assuming that the future will unfold magically into some contented state is naive. Often, individuals and couples don't have a good process for customizing decisions about their future choices of activity and places to live. Many new retirees think they'll be happy with unlimited leisure in a warm place, such as an Arizona desert or a Florida beach. They're in danger of becoming extremely disappointed when they get what they thought would make them happy. Personal wealth coaching provides an ongoing framework to continue to refine choices to invest in a profitable and fulfilling life.

Research shows that the lack of choices can lead to depression and despair. However, the most self-determined and wealthiest group of all, the rock-and-roll generation, is finding that the American dream of life, liberty, and the pursuit of happiness has an overload of options and choices for the future, which can lead to confusion and analysis paralysis. Personal wealth management, with the combination of a portfolio manager and a personal wealth coach, can help customize and narrow the field of choices in terms of what will truly bring profit and fulfillment to an investor's life.

> **Analysis paralysis:** An informal phrase applied to the condition when the opportunity cost of decision analysis exceeds the benefits.

In the book *The Paradox of Choice* (Ecco, 2004), Barry Schwartz helps us understand: "There is no denying that choice improves the quality of our lives. It enables us to control our destinies and to come close to getting exactly what we want out of any situation. Choice is essential to autonomy, which is absolutely fundamental to well-being. Healthy people want and need to direct their own lives." Later in his book, he points out that overwhelming numbers of choices and options can be debilitating. "On the other hand," he writes, "the fact that some choice is good doesn't necessarily mean that more choice is better. ... [T]here is a cost of having an overload of choice."

Just as the portfolio manager helps investors narrow the field of choices about their investment portfolios, the personal wealth coach provides a similar service in regard to choices about your personal wealth in total. Personal wealth coaching honors the need for investors to have autonomy by helping them make great choices about how to invest in their future lives. With a trained personal wealth coach, investors can make better decisions about a non-automatic future.

Coaching and the Visioning Process

Have you ever noticed that sometimes other people can envision something for you that you can't? Why is it that when you use a personal trainer at the gym, the trainer can often envision you working up to physical activities that you'd never dream of—like a long bike trip or running in a marathon? Coaches use their energy and enthusiasm to motivate their clients, often to visions well beyond what they dreamed. They can help you achieve what seems impossible.

People often tell me that they don't know how to vision, but visioning is easier than you may think. If I ask you to close your eyes right now and tell me what color shirt you're wearing, can you do it? If so, you can vision. Most people "see" a picture of the shirt in their mind's eye. Others don't; but if they know what color the shirt is, they vision in a nonvisual way. Some people call it remembering. You may call it sensing or feeling.

First, visioning creates a mental phenomenon called cognitive dissonance. Psychologists describe it as the discomfort you feel when you experience an inconsistency between your beliefs and your actions. When cognitive dissonance becomes unpleasant enough, it induces a drive state—you feel driven to reduce the dissonance by changing either your beliefs or your behaviors.

You may have read stories about wealthy people who've lost all their money and then quickly found ways to become wealthy again. Conversely, you've probably seen articles about lottery winners who rapidly spent or lost their winnings and went back to their previous financial level. They all experienced cognitive dissonance and changed their behaviors to match their beliefs.

Second, the human brain contains a cluster of cells known as the reticular activating system (RAS). This system acts as a filter, sorting out information and sending it to either your conscious or unconscious mind. Can you imagine what life would be like without such a system? Your conscious mind would be bombarded by every stimulus in your environment. You'd hear a sound and not know where to look first—at the chirping bird in a nearby tree, at the children playing in your neighbor's yard, or at the speeding car hurtling toward you.

Cognitive dissonance: The condition of conflict or anxiety resulting from inconsistency between your beliefs and your actions, such as believing that smoking is harmful but continuing to do it.

Reticular activating system: A network of structures, including the brain stem, medulla, thalamus, and nerve pathways, which function together to produce and maintain arousal.

Fortunately, the RAS filters out the unimportant, or at least puts it in the background. How does your RAS know the difference between what's important and what isn't? It uses your beliefs and values as guidelines. When you decide something's important, your RAS brings it to your attention. When you take time to envision a compelling future, your reticular activating system automatically focuses your attention on the information, opportunities, and resources to help bring that vision to life. This is especially true when you vision your future state of wisdom.

Let's try a brief exercise. Imagine the future you: a person who is healthy, wealthy, and wise. Even if you can't "see" this future you, get a feeling for that future person. Get a sense of your future self in a healthy, vibrant state. Now, what if "future you" could offer "present you" advice about decisions you're making now?

Many of my clients find this to be a powerful experience, as if they had an inner coach to offer words of wisdom and understanding as they make decisions. With regular practice, you too can improve your ability to make better decisions about your *life* portfolio, not just your financial portfolio. When most people envision the future, they tend to be overly optimistic about the realities they face. With the practice of visioning, you envision a future of wisdom to become someone who understands the true nature of wealth.

After you envision the ideal "future you," think about what you're doing today for your future self. Are you sending money ahead to this person? Are you sending health? Are you sending energy and optimism? Consider caring more for your future self by taking better care of your current life decisions.

The Greatest Treasure Hunt of Your Life

Imagine yourself on a majestic ship in search of buried treasure. What's the first thing you'll need? A map, of course. A compelling vision is the map to your life's destination. Once you know where you want to go, you can plot your course and prepare for dangers that might arise. With the wind in your sails and a sturdy main mast (your most cherished values), you'll be able to set short-term goals, develop timelines, and enjoy the journey. Upon arriving, you'll celebrate your good fortune and share it with others. The following questions will guide you on your treasure hunt:

- What are the possibilities of personal wealth for your life?
- What is your destiny?
- What old, ineffective patterns could sabotage your treasure hunt?
- Which of your most cherished values will sustain you on your treasure hunt?
- What measurable, achievable goals will you set, and what actions must you take to achieve them?
- How will you celebrate the treasures of your life?
- How will you use your treasure to serve others and make a difference?

Constructing the Future: It's Not Automatic!

It's easy to go through life on autopilot, earning money, advancing your career, putting food on the table, and reacting to challenges as they arise. Bill, a 61-year-old business owner, offered a great description of life before 50. "My goal was always to try to succeed in business," he said, "but when you get there, what do you do next? Where do you go? I don't think I've thought beyond the goal. If you ask a kid, 'What are you striving for?' he says, 'Well, I want to get out of college and I want to get a real good job.' Okay, then what? People don't always think beyond, until they're faced with it."

By the time you reach the half-century mark, you're probably well established in your career and community, your kids are grown or nearly so, and you finally have time to focus on yourself. For some people, the question, "Then what?" brings on a full-blown crisis. They start thinking life is almost over, and they get depressed because they haven't accomplished what they set out to do. Or worse, they buy into the negative stereotypes about aging and tell themselves, "It's all downhill from here," "The best part of life is behind me," and "It's too late to start anything new."

One benefit of a personal wealth coach is to counteract any negativity related to aging and to help investors seek prosperity by utilizing their talents long after their career-focused years are over. Last year, I met a couple named Joe and Sally. When Joe and Sally came for their initial coaching session, they both appeared tired. Even though they smiled politely, their faces were drawn, and I could see the worry. Joe wondered if he wanted to continue working as a physician.

We reviewed three questions I frequently ask my clients: "Who am I?" "Where am I going?" and "Who am I going with?" As we explored Joe and Sally's situation, it was clear they were focused on the question, "Who am I going with?" Joe thought perhaps he should look at other partnerships. Sally was also exploring options for herself that might lead to an exciting way to practice nursing. However, they were asking the questions backward! Rearranging the questions in the right order led to an amazing transformation.

When they explored "Who am I?" together, their energy dramatically picked up. The fatigue immediately lifted as they told their story about being trained in integrative medicine and their passion to help patients with these methods.

When I asked, "What are your passions outside of your work as a physician?" Joe cracked a smile and fumbled for something in his day planner. The smile spread across his face as he pulled out a picture. "Here you go," he said. "This is what I call a passion." I looked at the picture with surprise. It showed Joe riding at ninety miles an hour on a Ninja motorcycle, leaning through a curve with his knee scraping the road. "I've been racing motorcycles for a while now. I was thinking I might want to teach it some day," said Joe, before he broke into laughter. Sally laughed out loud with Joe, and suddenly the energy in the room increased.

Within a few subsequent sessions, it became obvious that numerous strengths and passions could help Joe and Sally discover a future life beyond Joe's current work as a physician. They made plans to market their work in integrative medicine, expanding the many possibilities of what their future purpose would be as a team at a new clinic they envisioned.

During each session, they were increasingly excited about their future years becoming their best years yet. Once they had rearranged their questions in the right order, amazing creativity about their future lives unfolded. They now have a business plan to work together to help patients be mentally prepared for surgery and to work in mind-body medicine. And Joe, at age 70, continues to race his Ninja motorcycle.

Of course, they also worked through all the issues of how to maximize their portfolio. We now have a vision and plan that relate to their current portfolio and will help them generate more income. Neither Joe nor Sally wants to retire into unlimited leisure. They want to be active and make a difference. Through the personal wealth management process, they now have a team approach for managing their personal wealth issues.

Personal wealth coaching provides a systematic method to explore critical life questions and integrate the answers into the revolutionary investor's approach to portfolio management. Personal wealth coaching is intentionally focused on visioning and creating a plan with milestones to accomplish. Revolutionary investors want profit. They want abundance. Often, however, investors are focused on scarcity, which can lead to poor choices and a lack of fulfillment.

Personal Wealth Management: The Key to a Worry-Free Tomorrow

When it comes to how we live our lives, we often don't know what lies ahead. The same applies to the discovery process of personal wealth coaching—you're always surprised. In both investing and in life, there are few total truths or quantifiable, foreseeable results. Most things revolve around probabilities: The better your process and the more thought-out it is, the higher the probability that you'll end up getting what you want. That's the driving factor behind personal wealth management, a valuable and proven process that keeps the revolutionary investor in mind.

Most people find it difficult to ease off, settle for the passenger seat, and rely on a proven process. They want to see forecasted results of where their portfolios will be, say, five years from now. But it's somewhat valueless to formulate a number and then offer it as truth (the higher the number, the better), because we're dealing with probabilities and not absolutes. Revolutionary investors have to come to grips with the idea that following a process, not chasing meaningless results, will get you where you want to go. You need to do the legwork, find the right advisor, and make sure that person is a professional who's right for you as a revolutionary investing in your own life. Once you've addressed every issue that's important to you—determining what it will take to make you complete as an individual—you need to relax, let the process work, and go on about your business.

My grandmother lived a very hard life. In all the years I knew her, I can't say she found any real peace of mind. She and my grandfather were a successful couple until 1929, living an upper-middle-class life. My grandmother's family owned sawmills and brick mills, and my grandfather managed a car dealership. For their young age, they were successful, dynamic people with a bright future.

In 1929, right before the infamous Wall Street crash, my grandfather—an energetic man in his mid-30s—had a heart attack and died suddenly. Following the death of her husband and the stock market crash, my grandmother was overwhelmed by the Great Depression years. In World War II, her son-in-law was killed; not long after, her daughter died of tuberculosis, leaving my grandmother to raise her grandchildren on an old farm owned by her father.

My grandmother's life changed dramatically in the course of a few years, and she had to persevere through a lot of awful things, which was par for the course in those difficult times. Because of this, her life was always plagued by worry. She often worried about the well-being of her grandkids. She felt the world was headed in a dark, terrible direction as the Cold War dawned. The forecast showed turbulent times ahead, and it was my grandmother's experience to expect the worst. And who could blame her?

Many people in the Greatest Generation have done well for themselves and have more money than they will ever need to spend. Even though you can mathematically show them that they have sufficient money to be financially independent for the rest of their lives, they're unceasingly worried about money. They have yet to make the connection between right-brain activity (how they spend the money) and the left-brain logistics that say there's a 99 percent probability they won't die poor and be a burden on those left behind. They can't make that connection, and therefore they can't find the peace of mind that comes with having a solid process, such as personal wealth management, in place.

You can have peace of mind in one of two ways: by being oblivious to what's going on around you, or by knowing you've done all you can to the best of your ability to plan for your future. As revolutionaries dedicated to finding the greatest possibilities our lives have to offer, we should strive for the latter. Like the natural satisfaction found in earning money in the first place, an informed, good feeling comes from knowing you've done all you can do to better your future. It's the idea that no stone has been left unturned, whatever happens from here will happen, a great process is in place, and probabilities suggest good things are on the way.

Here's the bottom line: You can get bogged down in your misfortunes when they arise, or you can address the pertinent issues to the best of your ability and move on. I don't spend much time contemplating what I'd do in an ice age oblivion following the meteor strike that scientists feel is bound to happen. I'm unable to change the outcome, so there's no use calculating what I'd do if it happened.

The whole purpose behind the personal wealth management ideas we've discussed in this chapter—be it the Wealth Management Benchmark, personal wealth coaching, or any other process—is to develop a high quality of life centered by peace of mind. It's important to rejuvenate investors' appreciation for what they've built and to help them feel confident that their hard work will pay off in the form of a better future for their family. Through the personal wealth management process, investors have a team approach for managing their personal wealth issues. In other words, the goal of personal wealth management is to help investors create a functional, healthy relationship between their money and their life.

Chapter 7

Risk Management in Today's Market

"The essence of investment management is the management of risks, not the management of returns."

—Benjamin Graham

A delightful woman—we'll call her Joan—had some concerns about her portfolio and asked me for advice. She had a substantial portfolio and many individualized needs, and the situation seemed overly complicated to her. Joan's advisor, who worked for a big Wall Street firm, had suggested that she use the firm's investment management consulting program. After exhaustive number crunching and projections based mainly on past performance, the firm determined that Joan needed twelve different portfolio managers—not three, not five, but twelve!—specializing in various styles. The intent was to diversify her portfolio, but the result was a highly complex mess.

Each of the twelve managers had his own personal approach or style to investing the assets delegated to him, and each invested in the same way for every client, with no customization of any kind. As a result, Joan had more than 530 different stocks. Because the right hand never knew what the left hand was doing, more than 70 were cross-owned in varying amounts by the different portfolio managers. On top of that, Joan's portfolio included several hundred different bond issues.

I could write an entire book about how many things were wrong with the investment-consulting approach that Joan's advisor used. Her monthly statements exceeded 250 pages, as did her tax returns. And sadly, she was paying through the nose for this less-than-rewarding experience. She met with her advisor on a quarterly basis, and he presented an exhaustive report outlining everything that had occurred in each of her accounts, as well as the quarterly performance of each manager compared to almost every market benchmark index known to humanity. Joan always left trying to figure out what it all meant. She once asked me, "Why did my financial consultant do this to me?" I replied, "It's not that he did it to you, it's the idea that Wall Street firms have only standard-ized products and a limited ability to customize portfolios for an individual's needs."

In today's changing world, where markets constantly fluctuate and individuals have different needs and goals, Wall Street's con-ventional approach is to create a different product to deal with each specific environment. The more environments we have, the more and different types of products they create. Each one is style spe-cific, meaning it's intended to deal with a specific environment and will go in and out of favor over time as the environment changes.

If markets were *not* dynamic and ever-changing, we would need only one methodology to deal with them: whatever makes the most money. For example, if stocks made the most money, then we could have an asset allocation of 100 percent stocks and never change it. In effect, we would have a riskless market without any fluctuation. Whichever asset class had the highest return would always be best. If that were the case, investing would be a simple single choice. In reality, things are much more complicated.

Asset: A resource having economic value that an individual, corporation, or country owns or controls with the expectation that it will provide future benefit.

Asset allocation: The process of dividing a portfolio among major asset classes such as stocks, bonds, and cash.

Efficient portfolio: A portfolio that earns the highest return with the least amount of volatility.

Because the environment is always changing, the worst way to choose the investment product that will do best in the future is to select the one that had the highest overall return in the past. The only way you could expect success with that method would be if the environment was static in the future, which we know isn't the case. That's why Wall Street's approach has not done very well: Their products work, but they perform best in certain specific environments—and, at the extreme, they can backfire and blow up on you in the wrong environment.

Today's investors are dealing with a dynamic market environment. The more dynamic the environment, the more tools you need to deal with the changes. A changing environment with many tools (investment products, securities, risk management methods, and so on) needs a dynamic process to manage tool selection. To not only weather but take advantage of the different market cycles, you need a process that utilizes the right tools for the current environment To date, Wall Street has done a poor job of making that transition, instead specializing in producing standardized products without a process that is sufficiently dynamic to adjust to the ever-changing markets.

It amazes me that so many investors are willing to plunk down tens of thousands of dollars in investments that they barely understand, with no meaningful process for managing their investments through treacherous waters. Before you can create a profitable investment program, you need a good education in the fundamentals of investing. This chapter will teach you the basics behind a winning portfolio strategy, whether you choose to invest on your own or delegate your investment activities to a trusted portfolio manager. You'll learn several crucial concepts, including how to recognize and manage the different types of risk, how to deal with market fluctuation and volatility, and how to build an efficient portfolio through proper diversification and asset allocation. Then, in the next chapter, you'll learn a revolutionary new process for using the right tools at the right times.

Managing Risk: The Key to Successful Investing

The single most important key to successful portfolio management is the ability to manage risk. If you can't manage risk, you can't manage the outcome.

Let me ask you a question: How would you define risk? People usually define it as the likelihood that the value of an investment could drop in price and, in some cases, not go back up or lose money. However, that answer defines only one type of risk: market risk. Unfortunately, there are several types of investment risk, and they all affect the return on your investment in some way.

A broader definition of risk includes the following:

- *Market risk* arises from the fluctuating prices of investments as they're traded in global markets. It includes loss of principal, fluctuations in investment price, and lack of liquidity (the inability to sell an investment when you want to). If market risk were the only type of risk you needed to worry about, it would make sense to invest only in certificates of deposit (CDs), U.S. Treasury bills (T-bills), and money markets, because they're not subject to market risk. Unfortunately, they're subject to other types of risk.

- *Event risk* involves an unforeseen and abrupt shock that arises from a general risk such as a natural disaster, company default, technology failure, human error, political upheaval, or war. For example, the S&P 500 index dropped more than 11 percent in the eleven days after the events of 9/11.

- *Inflation risk* is the loss of purchasing power over a period of time; it forces you to spend more money over time to maintain the lifestyle to which you're accustomed. Your personal inflation rate may be higher than the government-quoted rate, based on how you spend your money. Most people will agree that it costs much more to live today than it did ten or fifteen years ago.

- *Tax risk* is the impact of investment taxes on investment return. For example, if investment income is taxable, individuals in the highest tax bracket lose a significant percentage of the total income earned on their investments. In addition, they have to pay capital gains tax on realized gains when their investments are sold.

- *Reinvestment risk* occurs when the proceeds from maturing securities like bonds may not be reinvested at the same rate at which they were initially invested. Grandma and Grandpa thought they would be financially independent when they invested their money in CDs in 1981 at 14 percent. Unfortunately, interest rates have declined throughout the years since that time. Today, they could invest at about 4 or 5 percent. Another example is that most investors profited from the 20-plus percent returns of the stock market from 1995 through 1999. The history of the market indicates that returns will most likely be less in the future. Retirees who locked in high interest rates on bonds in the late '90s will be able to renew those bonds at only about half the original interest rate.

- *Opportunity risk* occurs when people miss a chance to take a path that could lead to higher net worth. For example, by overestimating their need for readily available cash, they may miss the opportunity to invest in something that could generate high returns.

- *Psychological risk* is associated with feelings of fear and greed. Many people tend to get too optimistic (greedy) when markets go up; they put too large a percentage of their assets in risky investments when times are good. On the other hand, when markets decline, people experience fear, which causes them to pull money out at the bottom of the market. Because people generally feel bad at the bottom and good at the top, an emotion-based investment process is largely doomed from the start; emotional investors add to and pull out their money in the market at the wrong times. People who practice this method rarely do well in their investing over the long term.

- *Procrastination risk* reflects the lost opportunity that results from not taking action at the proper time. Because of uncertainty about which action to take, procrastinators avoid making decisions and do nothing. Procrastination also occurs when you fail to recognize the importance of taking immediate action. Procrastination can also come from a lack of confidence arising from an insufficient basic understanding of investment management principles.

The Myth of "Risk-Free" Investments

Occasionally, some of my clients ask me to buy safe or "risk-free" investments for them. I can't do it, because a risk-free investment doesn't exist. It can't exist. An investment may be free of one or even two types of risk, but it can't avoid the effects of all types of risk. For example, T-bill returns have pretty much averaged the inflation rate after taxes. Because they tend to mirror inflation, they're free from market risk but greatly affected by inflation risk. Other types of bonds, such as 30-year government bonds, have more market risk than T-bills and thus justify a slightly higher return over time. Corporate bonds have a little more risk than government bonds and consequently produce an even higher return. Bonds are subject to inflation risk because the interest they pay stays the same: They aren't indexed to inflation, and they mature at the same amount for which they were originally issued, thus entailing inflation risk.

The relationship between market risk and total return also holds for stocks. The S&P 500 generates a much higher return over the long run than a fixed-income security like a bond or T-bill. Small cap stocks, which represent new or relatively young companies, generate the highest return among stocks after inflation because they carry the highest amount of risk.

Market Capitalization

Stocks are often referred to as large cap or small cap. These designations refer to the market capitalization, or market value, of the companies. Typically, the categories are as follows:

Mega cap $200 billion+
Large cap $10 billion–$200 billion
Mid cap $2 billion–$10 billion
Small cap $300 million–$2 billion
Micro cap $50 million–$300 million

Mega and large caps are the blue chips, and micro caps are penny stocks.

Simply put, a relationship exists between risk and return. Taking no risk leads to receiving no real return. Sounds fair, doesn't it? A person who wants to avoid all risk will ultimately end up losing money as it relates to purchasing power. On the other hand, taking on more risk can result in higher returns as well as a higher possibility for losses. Investing in a portfolio of high-risk securities can lead to high negative returns. This happens because risky securities tend to fluctuate more, resulting in a large loss when the securities fall out of favor. Such a loss can be so great that the investor can't recover and recoup the losses.

Managing Market Fluctuation: Efficient Market Theory

In figure 7.1, which investment would you rather own: Investment A, with a 10 percent return, or Investment B, with a 3 percent return? Of course, you'd select Investment A. Everyone would. There's only one problem—it doesn't exist.

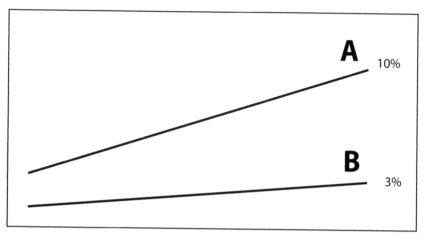

FIGURE 7.1 Portfolio A: Not an option

In reality, to get a higher rate of return, you have to deal with some degree of price fluctuation. This concept, known as efficient market theory, is illustrated in figure 7.2. Efficient market theory states that there is a relationship between risk, or price fluctuation, and return. More fluctuation should justify a higher rate of return, but it takes a longer amount of time to reach an average expected return. Conversely, with only a little fluctuation, the return will be less but will be more predictable.

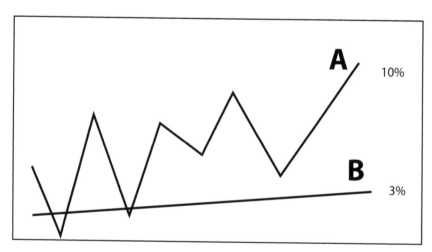

FIGURE 7.2 Fluctuation vs. growth

Think for a moment about your savings account—your nest egg in the local bank. Savings accounts are always liquid, always available for life's short-term needs. Investments, however, are made with a longer time horizon in mind. That's why you can expect a higher return on an investment than you can get from a non-fluctuating savings account. Although some less-liquid investments don't reveal fluctuation as obviously, it does exist. In real estate, for example, you typically buy a property and then sell it years later. Generally, you sell it for more than you paid. However, if you had to find a buyer every day for that piece of real estate, you would see a great deal of fluctuation in the price. The same would be true if you had direct ownership of a company. Assuming the company was profitable, the value would probably go up over time; but if you had to find a buyer for it every day, you would notice the daily fluctuation.

Liquidity: The ability to convert an asset to cash quickly. Also known as marketability.

In the same way, market fluctuation doesn't necessarily mean a loss or gain of principal. It's just fluctuation—the ups and downs that markets have. The value of your portfolio one year ago, today, or one year in the future is irrelevant. (The exception is when you experience a very large decrease in principal. Such declines indicate poor diversification or an investment strategy that's weak in risk management.) That said, the only time the value of an account really matters is when you begin to spend the money, or if you have to liquidate your entire portfolio to meet some kind of need. Because the goal of most investors isn't to wipe out their entire investment portfolios, it makes good sense to invest for the long term and benefit from the higher returns that result from fluctuation.

Diversification: Holding a collection of independent assets in order to reduce overall risk.

Efficient market theory: An economic theory that states that there is a relationship between risk, or price fluctuation, and return. More fluctuation should justify a higher rate of return, but it takes a longer amount of time to reach an average expected return. Conversely, with only a little fluctuation, the return will be less but will be more predictable.

Remember the concept of psychological risk? It's the risk undisciplined investors face, causing them to panic during down periods and liquidate their portfolios at the bottom. Don't get emotional about market fluctuations. Remember, fluctuation in price isn't the same as losing money. With investments, you'll have good days and bad days. Periods of stellar performance and periods of underperformance are inevitable, but basing your investment decisions on these short-term periods is a recipe for disaster.

Bad days, or down days, can actually enhance returns over time. Good portfolio managers use processes to manage volatility, or large fluctuations in the market. Their portfolios tend to drop less than the market when it goes down. Then, when the market rebounds, they're coming off a higher base, so they make more money and have less fluctuation. They also know the importance of being concerned about big advances over a short period of time, because those indicate a portfolio that's not properly diversified. Big advances over a short period should eventually result in big losses in the future. A well-diversified portfolio should ratchet its way up in a measured fashion and ultimately make more money. If a portfolio manager doesn't manage volatility well, then the portfolio can take large hits in value that are hard to recover. With good portfolio management, you can get solid returns with fewer fluctuations.

Somewhere in the future, the value of the market will be higher than it is today. In the meantime, fluctuations will occur. There can be more advantages than disadvantages to having fluctuation in a portfolio. Fluctuation is the price you pay for liquidity, and liquidity gives you the ability to make timely adjustments within your portfolio. For example, if you had invested heavily in Enron, WorldCom, or a similar dog with fleas, you would have had the option to use a sell discipline to cut those losers from your portfolio and reinvest the proceeds into securities with more potential to make money. Managed fluctuation can enhance your returns over the long run.

Modern Portfolio Theory

You've already learned that, for a single asset class (such as stocks or real estate), more risk generally leads to a greater return over time. Is there any way to alter the risk-return equation and get a higher return while taking lower risk? Nobel Prize winner Harry Markowitz, the father of modern portfolio theory, says yes.

More than fifty years ago, before the widespread use of computers, Markowitz observed that you can reduce a portfolio's volatility by combining investments with different patterns of return. In *Asset Allocation* (McGraw-Hill, 2000), author Roger C. Gibson explains Markowitz's approach:

> *Before modern portfolio theory, investment management was a two-dimensional process focusing primarily on the volatility and return characteristics of individual securities. As a result of Harry Markowitz's work, recognition grew regarding the importance of the interrelationships among securities within portfolios. Modern portfolio theory added a third dimension to portfolio management that evaluates a security's diversification effect on a portfolio. This term refers to the impact that the inclusion of a particular asset class or security will have on the volatility and return characteristics of the overall portfolio.*

Modern portfolio theory thus shifted the focus of attention away from individual securities and toward a consideration of the portfolio as a whole.

Diversification effect: The impact that the inclusion of a particular asset class or security has on the volatility and return characteristics of the overall portfolio.

Modern portfolio theory says that you can generate a higher return with lower portfolio fluctuation—if the investments in your portfolio work together. One of the basics behind this theory is the attempt to create an efficient portfolio, one that earns the highest return with the least amount of volatility. This can be accomplished by owning a diverse group of securities that fluctuate in different ways.

The main concern associated with market fluctuation is lack of diversification. If you had put all your money in Enron and continued to ride it (thus practicing the buy-and-hold investment method), you would have lost that money. It wouldn't have mattered how long you waited—you wouldn't have gotten your money back in Enron. However, if you follow the principles of diversification and managing volatility, your portfolio should trend upward over time, following the lead of typical markets, which usually trend up. The exception? A catastrophic event such as a serious war breaking out in some country, resulting in the end of a political regime and that country's market becoming nationalized or ceasing to exist. In almost all other situations, markets trend up over time.

Let's All Move Together Now

Proper diversification refers to the way individual securities fluctuate in relationship to each other. However, it's important to note that the correlation among different securities can range from high to low. Figure 7.3 shows a high positive correlation among four securities; let's suppose they are Texaco, ExxonMobil, Chevron, and British Petroleum. As you can see from the chart, all four stocks are affected by the same things; they have a high positive correlation. If oil prices go down, the prices of all four stocks go down. If oil prices go up, all four stocks' prices tend to go up. In this example, the fluctuation over time should justify about an average 10 percent rate of return.

> **Correlation:** A statistical measure of how two securities move in relation to each other.

The chart illustrates that the benefit from diversifying among four stocks with high positive correlation is limited. You could achieve the same diversification by owning just two of these stocks instead of four. Securities with high positive correlation within a portfolio don't achieve the benefit expected through diversification.

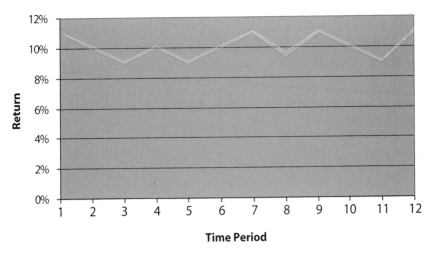

FIGURE 7.3 Positive correlation

Figure 7.4 is an example of two securities that have a high negative correlation. The two stocks are affected by the same events but in the opposite way. For example, the lighter line could represent Texaco from the previous chart, and the darker line could represent a transportation company that uses oil, such as FedEx.

As you can see in Figure 7.4, a drop in oil prices would be bad for the oil inventories at Texaco but good for FedEx, whose many planes and trucks require fuel. It's reasonable to think that both FedEx and Texaco stocks could be profitable over the long term, but most of the time they tend not to fluctuate together because they're affected by the same events in opposite ways. In this example, both securities have the same (but opposite) fluctuation, and both should generate a 10 percent rate of return. In other words, a portfolio of both securities would average a 10 percent return with little fluctuation. However, in the real world, it's not possible to achieve true negative correlation among securities over the long term.

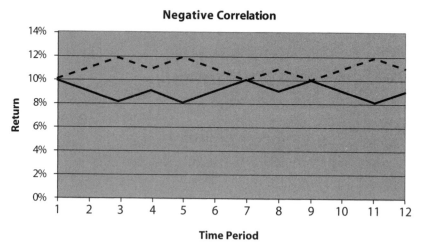

FIGURE 7.4 Negative correlation

Figure 7.5 shows a typical real-world portfolio with a high degree of randomness (no correlation) among its securities. Each security in the portfolio has a similar degree of volatility and should justify about a 10 percent rate of return. As you can see, some did very well and some did not. The dashed line represents the portfolio as a whole. The portfolio averaged about 10 percent—the average return of each individual security—but had only a fraction of the fluctuation of the individual securities. In other words, the higher rate of volatility of the individual securities, combined with the fact that there was almost no correlation among them, gave this portfolio a high rate of return with low risk. The risk was greatly reduced because of the low correlation among the individual stocks.

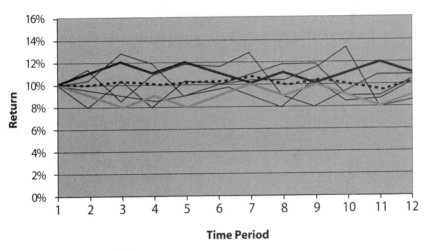

FIGURE 7.5 Portfolio management

The Good, the Bad, and the Diversified

The stock market, by definition, is diversified. The risk associated with the market as a whole is called systematic or market-related risk. Market-related risk means that when the market goes up or down, it affects most individual securities in the same direction. If the market goes up 3 percent in one day, most individual stocks also go up.

Individual stocks, by definition, aren't diversified. The risk associated with individual stocks is called unsystematic or stock-specific risk. For example, the general market may rise; but, for whatever reason, an individual stock may go down. Movement in a stock's price is related more to the stock than to the market as a whole. A stock may go in an entirely different direction than the market or move more dramatically than the market.

> **Mutual fund:** A security that gives investors access to a portfolio of equities, bonds, and other securities. Each shareholder participates in the gain or loss of the fund. Shares are issued and can be redeemed as needed.
>
> **Systematic/market-related risk:** The risk inherent to the entire market or entire market segment. This is undiversifiable risk.
>
> **Unsystematic/stock-specific risk:** Risk that affects a small number of stocks. For example, news that is specific to a small number of stocks, such as a sudden strike by the employees of a company you have shares in, is considered to be unsystematic risk.

It's important to know that stock-specific risk can be diversified away. However, efficient markets don't pay a premium return for risk that can be diversified away. As a result, investors aren't paid a premium return for taking a risk that could have been lessened by diversifying. The bottom line is that you should properly diversify your portfolio.

You may be surprised to know that diversifying mutual funds doesn't have the same risk-lowering effect as diversifying individual securities, because each mutual fund owns many securities. It's true that most funds have just about eliminated the individual security risk, and that mutual funds are primarily subject to market-specific risk or to the risk of the fund manager's specific investment style. However, if a portfolio contains several mutual funds, they have a higher correlation among each other, which is why you benefit less from diversifying among several mutual funds.

Understanding how securities correlate, or move in relationship with one another, is a critical component in proper diversification. In our earlier example of negative correlation, you saw that an oil company's stock and a transportation company's stock generally move in opposite directions as a result of shared economic circumstances. If oil prices go up, it's usually good for the oil company but bad for the transportation company. Both companies' stocks may be good long-term investments, but in the short term, one should underperform. You also learned that a better scenario is to invest in stocks that move up and down independently, or with random correlation. For instance, the stock price of a manufacturing company producing motors for washing machines in Newark, New Jersey, probably won't be impacted by the same market conditions that affect the stock price of a company that owns twenty fast-food restaurants in Hong Kong. Both stocks may go up or down at the same time, but not because there's a relationship between the two. With a portfolio of unrelated securities, you can make more money with less risk during volatile market fluctuations.

One question people tend to ask is how many stocks they should own in a portfolio. Generally speaking, the variance associated with owning one stock is almost 50 percent. This means if you own only one stock, your portfolio is likely to go up or down by as much as 50 percent in one year. However, investing money in two stocks that aren't in the same industry should reduce your portfolio's risk to a little over 25 percent. Investing in three stocks decreases the risk even more, and each additional stock continues to reduce the risk, but by a smaller amount. You can continue to decrease risk by adding more stocks to your portfolio until you accumulate fifteen to twenty unrelated stocks. At this point, your portfolio should have more than 90 percent of the diversification of the market. Adding additional stocks to your portfolio will have only a minimal effect on risk reduction—in fact, adding more stocks will ultimately begin to water down the impact of the individual stocks. Keep in mind that the stocks in this example have low correlations with each other.

Variance: A measure of the dispersion of a set of data points around their mean value. Variance is a mathematical expectation of the average squared deviations from the mean. Variance measures the variability or volatility from an average. Volatility is a measure of risk, so this statistic can help determine the risk an investor might take on when purchasing a specific security.

Making Market Volatility Work for You

Let me give you a simple example of how market volatility can work for you. The following chart demonstrates how you can make money from fluctuation. It shows how two different portfolios work during market fluctuations.

	Portfolio A Nondiversified Portfolio	Portfolio B Diversified Portfolio
Investment	$100	$100
Loss	50%	25%
Value	$50	$75
Gain	100%	50%
Net	$100	$112.50
Percentage Return	0%	12.5%

Investor A, seeking maximum return, concentrates his securities in stocks that have similar characteristics (Portfolio A). Investor B wants to spread the risk, so she buys a diversified mix of securities from different investment classes, such as domestic stocks, bonds, international securities, and real estate (Portfolio B). Each portfolio is originally worth $100.

Suppose these portfolios experience a bear market, which is defined as a market in which prices drop or correct by 20 percent or more. During the bear market, Portfolio A loses 50 percent of its value. That kind of sharp loss can easily occur in a portfolio that has very little diversification. Investor A is left with just $50, meaning he'll have to make a 100 percent gain in the future just to be back where he started.

What happens to Portfolio B during the bear market? Again, Investor B starts with a $100 investment. However, because her portfolio is diversified among different investment classes, it's only half as volatile as Portfolio A. Thus, the bear market causes Portfolio B to drop only 25 percent (half as much as Portfolio A), leaving Investor B with $75.

Eventually the market rises again, sending Portfolio A up 100 percent to recoup the original loss, and sending Portfolio B up by 50 percent ($37.50)—only half as much as Portfolio A, because of the greater diversity. However, Investor B now has $112.50 in her portfolio. The difference is a zero return versus a 12.5 percent return, and the 12.5 percent return required only half the fluctuation.

As strange as it may sound, the risk that most people are afraid of—market volatility—can help enhance your return. Portfolio B made more money than Portfolio A because B dropped less when the market went down. It also went up less when the market rose, but it ended up with a higher return because the advance occurred from a bigger base ($75 instead of $50). I call this the ratchet effect: The more volatile the market, the more the diversified portfolio's return is enhanced. A diversified portfolio should grow because it benefits from not falling with the market.

Although this is a simple example of how modern portfolio theory works, it may be the most important concept you'll learn in this chapter. It shows that it's possible to get high returns with low risk. Managing volatility in your portfolio is critical to having a successful long-term investment program.

I can't emphasize this enough—**you don't have to take more risk to make more money!** One of the goals of the diversified portfolio is to benefit from volatility and achieve more consistent returns than typical stock or bond indices. Having more consistent returns makes it possible to make more money over time with less risk—the key ingredient in achieving successful lifelong performance.

Putting It All Together

Now that you've been introduced to the concepts of risk and modern portfolio theory, how can you make them work for you? The answer is surprisingly simple: Diversify your holdings by owning uncorrelated securities, and add time. Remember that time is the magic ingredient for successful investing. Two of the most important aspects of a winning portfolio-management strategy are patience and discipline. Both involve using time to your advantage and keeping your emotions in check:

- *You need patience to give the market time to endure its cycles.* The best investment results are achieved over time, rather than immediately. Quality investments held for a suitable time almost always produce good returns.

- *You need discipline to focus on long-term results.* If you've constructed your portfolio and continue to manage it to minimize risk, then you should ignore the temptation to fix a short-term setback by changing the process or buying the latest hot stock touted by the popular financial media.

This second component—discipline—needs to be emphasized. The biggest risk people face in managing their investments doesn't come from the market; it comes from allowing their emotions to circumvent the investment process.

When you wake up one morning and realize that your portfolio's value has dropped, your emotions tell you to sell. If you do, your losses become permanent, and you won't be in the market when it goes back up. As you learned earlier in this chapter, we call this psychological risk. It's what happens when you let your emotions replace strong investment discipline.

Money tends to be an emotional subject. It may seem easy today to say you're investing for long-term results. However, it may not be so easy tomorrow if the Dow Jones Industrial Average drops 500 points, or the market moves downward by 10 percent or more, or if rising interest rates cause bonds to decline.

To make matters worse, you're constantly bombarded by news stories about the current state of the market. Most of this financial analysis is short-term oriented. For example, if the market is down one day, the media will likely say the Dow "plunged" and offer three or four reasons why it happened. When the market is up, the media will interview experts who give specific advice on how to thrive in current market conditions, especially recommending stocks that are doing well at the moment. In short, the media focuses primarily on what's happening now or in the past, instead of trying to teach people how to follow a disciplined investment approach.

There will always be people with a narrowly focused investment strategy who happen to be in the right place at the right time. They'll make huge returns today, and they'll be covered by the media. If you listen to their advice, you'll be chasing the hot portfolio manager or mutual fund after it's already gone up; more often than not, you'll be buying at the top. What you won't hear is that, ultimately, investments that have the highest returns also have the greatest losses. The cause of the quick rise for a hot performer will also be the cause for its ultimate demise. Proper portfolio management is about consistency in returns and managing risk, not hitting home runs.

My advice is simple: Don't get investment advice from the media. News articles that engender feelings of fear or greed often lead to portfolio adjustments that seem satisfying in the short term but may have negative consequences in the future. By the time information reaches the media, it's already been reflected in the price of the market. The media's job should be to report financial news rather than make specific stock recommendations.

Here are three more points to help you keep emotion out of your investment decisions:

- *The best defense against emotional investing is knowledge.* You don't need to become an expert at portfolio management and the stock and bond markets, but it's important to learn the fundamentals and adopt a rules-based system for investment management. Once you have a process that meets your objectives, make only small adjustments, even if the process is currently out of favor.

- *When short-term results are disappointing, don't panic.* Remember that a well-diversified portfolio fluctuates over time, so declines are generally temporary and should eventually turn into gains. That said, your portfolio shouldn't have large short-term fluctuations. If it does, then you probably aren't properly diversified. A diversified portfolio has the virtue of consistency, losing a little today, gaining a little tomorrow—one step back, two steps forward. Over time, by avoiding the extremes, such a portfolio will always achieve the best investment results.

- *Have the discipline to stay focused on long-term success.* As the old saying goes, if it ain't broke, don't fix it. Don't worry too much about the month-to-month fluctuations in your portfolio's value. Fluctuations shouldn't be considered gains or losses of principal. Fluctuations are just fluctuations and are the cost of liquidity. Be sure your portfolio manager is protecting against large drops that are hard to recover. Over the long term, a diversified portfolio will grow at a fairly consistent rate with a minimum of risk.

Market Timing: Good or Bad Idea?

If stocks sometimes increase greatly and other times decrease greatly, why can't you continually reshuffle your portfolio, moving money heavily into stocks when their price is low, waiting until they increase, and then selling them? In other words, why can't you time the market, buying low and selling high? Market timing means trying to be in the market when it goes up and trying to get out of the market when it goes down. It's a great idea, but it's very difficult to do. (How many rich day traders do you know?)

The problem is that stocks don't behave in a consistent manner. Stock prices generally go up and down in sharp spikes over a short period of time. To make things worse, these spikes usually happen when people least expect them. For example, take the Persian Gulf War and the Y2K scare. Most people predicted that each of these occurrences would drive the stock market way down. However, the exact opposite happened: The market went up during both time periods. On March 24, 2000, the S&P 500 registered its highest high at 1527; and on October 9, 2002, it registered its lowest low at 776.75.

On December 31, 1999, we all watched when clocks struck midnight in New Zealand, signaling Y2K. And nothing happened! Later that evening, at a New Year's Eve party, I was sitting on the couch watching Dick Clark on TV. Two young men sat down next to me and began discussing their plans to make lots of money in their Internet stocks, now that Y2K had been a bust and nothing stood in their way. "This is a new paradigm, man. We won't have bear markets like we did in the old days. Baby boomers have to save for retirement, so lots of money will be going into their 401(k)s and will need to be invested. The new Information Age and Internet will change the way we do everything. Tech stocks are the only way to go. Just buy them whenever they dip in price; they will only go higher."

Internet stocks were already through the roof, and I told my young friends that parabolic advances always end the same way—with parabolic drops. The sharp decline was sure to happen; it was only a matter of when. I agreed that the Internet would change everything and that we were entering a new age, but I warned, "Don't confuse companies with stocks. They are two totally different things."

Stocks, markets, and other financial securities go up and down for only one reason: the irrefutable law of supply and demand. For the price to go up, more people need to be initiating buys than sells. For the price to go down, more people need to initiate sells than buys. It's that simple. Supply and demand are primarily determined by human emotion. The only reason people are willing to initiate a buy is because they think the stock will be worth more in the future. This truth leads to the counterintuitive nature of markets. When everyone thinks the market is going up, it probably will go down. When you're convinced that the market is going down, it generally goes up.

There's a reason for the madness, as illustrated by the Internet stock bubble of 2000. By the time the vast majority of investors thought Internet stocks were going up, most of those people who wanted to invest in them had already done so, which meant there wasn't much money left to buy more and cause the price to go higher. Stockholders expected to double their money over a short period of time, but their expectations couldn't continue to be met over the long term. As buying slowed, so did the advances. The "hot money" got discouraged and began to move elsewhere. When the advance began to stall, people with money to invest were less likely to buy Internet stocks, and people who already held Internet stocks wanted to sell and keep some of their profits.

Sharp advances have one thing in common: They're always followed by sharp declines. The higher and faster a security goes up, the more euphoric people become. When the stock eventually fails to meet expectations, everyone heads for the door at the same time. As a result, the majority of investors will eventually be wrong. During most of 1999, it was commonly believed that the stock market would go down in the fourth quarter, prior to Y2K. The reality was that almost all the money made in 1999 was made in the fourth quarter.

That's why it's not a good idea to take market timing to an extreme, meaning getting totally in or out of the market. As a matter of fact, it's not a good idea to use any investment-management technique to the extreme. If you or your portfolio manager has a process to predict the direction of the market, and you have reason to believe that the process will be right more often than wrong over the long term, then it's okay to do some market timing on a limited basis. But keep in mind that you can never be sure you're right. Making big changes in your asset allocation isn't a good idea. If you miss the spikes in the market, even by a few days, you won't make even an average return on your investment, much less a premium return. To make things worse, you never know when those few critical days will occur.

Asset Allocation: A Balancing Act

Asset allocation has to do with how your portfolio is diversified among the three major asset classes: stocks, bonds, and cash. The addition of stocks, bonds, and cash diversifies your portfolio; but if you're like most investors, keeping track of all these components can get a little confusing. Here are a few fundamentals to help you manage and understand asset allocation:

- Adding bonds to your stock portfolio meets one of the requirements of proper diversification because stocks and bonds generally have low correlation with each other. Stocks and bonds tend to move in opposite directions when the market is volatile.

- When people get concerned about the stock market, they tend to sell their stocks and move their money to bonds, thus making the bond market go up.

- A portfolio contains two different types of cash: The first is called a living fund, which includes all the money you need for your upcoming expenses. The second is called tactical cash, and it's used to manage volatility. If both the stock market and the bond market are unsettled, you can reduce your portfolio's volatility by increasing the amount of tactical cash in it.

Conventional wisdom dictates that your asset allocation—the percentage of cash, stocks, and bonds—should remain relatively the same over time. This idea was created to prevent investors from changing their asset allocation based on psychological risk. Changes in asset allocation were considered attempts to time the market. However, most people do the opposite when trying to time the market.

Here's an example to consider: An investor has 80 percent of his portfolio in stocks, and then the market goes down. He feels uncomfortable with the downward market fluctuation (as do most normal human beings) and decides to sell a portion of his stocks until he feels comfortable again. He changes his asset allocation to, say, 40 percent stocks. But it's important to remember that the market has already gone down. As a result, the investor who had 80 percent stocks when the stock market went down will have only 40 percent when the market ultimately rebounds to its former level.

The psychology of investing urges most people to get optimistic at peaks and pessimistic at bottoms. Changing their asset allocation based on the emotions of fear and greed may cause them to be at the wrong place at the wrong time. Therefore, most investment experts recommend keeping the same asset allocation all the time. I disagree with their philosophy, and I'll explain why in the next chapter.

Most of the fundamentals of portfolio management and successful investing covered in this chapter are time-tested truths. For example, you learned that volatility in the market can be a good thing when you have an efficient, diversified portfolio. You discovered that a diversified portfolio of stocks won't normally go up as fast or fall as fast as the market, meaning that a diversified portfolio results in more money over time because its fluctuations aren't as severe as those of the market. Even during market declines, a well-diversified portfolio will maintain a higher value and be poised to benefit from the next up market. You also learned that stock diversification works even better when you add bonds and cash to your portfolio. And you learned that efficient markets are fairly priced and should pay a premium return versus the risk taken.

However, despite these fundamental truths, and given that markets are generally efficient, most investors haven't had the success you might expect. The truth is that the Information Age has changed the playing field. Technology has made information available more quickly than ever before. New systems, methodologies, and tools are being developed to deal with the complexities of this ever-changing market, and the revolutionary investor needs to take advantage of these tools just to keep up.

Chapter 8

The Revolutionary Investment Process

"We live in an era of revolution—the revolution of rising expectations."

—Adlai Stevenson

Imagine a big factory that is the number-one cog producer in the world. It's so big that if for some reason this factory didn't produce cogs, the ripple effect on the world's economy would be devastating. One day, the gigantic machine that produces cogs breaks. Management summons a number of engineers to try to fix the cog machine—all to no avail, so they call the world's greatest cog machine expert. When he arrives, he reaches into his enormous toolbox, containing many complicated, high-tech tools, and selects a huge hammer. The expert walks up to the machine, eyes a particular spot, and hits the machine three times as hard as he can. A puff of smoke comes out of the machine, and cogs start rolling down the line again. The expert bills the cog company $50,000.

Six months later, the cog machine breaks again. The company president, nonplussed with the previous $50,000 hammer job, finds a big hammer and hits the machine in the same spot. A few sparks come out of the machine, but no cogs. He summons the cog machine expert. This time, the expert reaches into his toolbox and pulls out a Phillips-head screwdriver. He sticks his screwdriver in the machine and rattles it around, and cogs begin coming out of the machine. The cog expert gives the president another bill for $50,000.

The president grumbles, gives the expert a check, and says, "I'm really confused. I hit the machine with a hammer in the same spot you did, but it didn't work." The cog guru says, "I have a number of tools. Each is designed to address a specific need. Using the wrong tool for the wrong need can have a disastrous effect. Knowing the right tool for the right place at the right time costs $50,000."

We all know that expertise has value. However, it's not just about having a lot of tools. It's about having an expert select the appropriate tool at the right time to deal with a specific problem. Whether it's a cog machine or your portfolio, fixing problems requires different tools and, more important, a dynamic process for matching the tools to the specific problem. What does this mean to revolutionary investors? As you shift the way you think about your money—and how you invest your money—you'll find that the revolutionary investment process requires matching the right tools (say, securities and investment products) to solve the problem in a dynamic environment.

Why Traditional Methods No Longer Work

In the last chapter, we discussed some fundamental principles for portfolio management—among them, the facts that securities fluctuate, and all fluctuating securities don't move up and down together. Those two facts mean that markets and securities are dynamic and ever changing. John M. Mulvey, Ph.D., a professor at Princeton University, states, "Markets are dynamic and should be addressed as such, rather than via static, single-period approaches."

Dynamic markets:

- Require a process that can adjust to changing market environments

- Require many tools—in this case, many different kinds of securities and investment products—to deal with changing market environments

Unfortunately, traditional or conventional methods can't meet these needs. That's because:

- Traditional brokerage firms and financial advisors focus on which specific securities or investment products to buy instead of on a meaningful *process* for managing them all.

- Traditional methods are, well, traditional. They haven't incorporated new techniques, such as customization, that are wanted by today's investors who are leading the revolution.

- Traditional approaches include either passive investing (generally indexing) or a limited style-specific active investment process using a few tools with a limited ability to change them.

The Information Age has created the opportunity to develop revolutionary approaches to manage and customize portfolios. Today's revolutionary investor can defy conventional wisdom and follow the advice of Frank Armstrong, the founder of Investor Solutions, Inc. Frank writes:

Conventional wisdoms can continue to influence our behavior in spite of overwhelming, abundant, and irrefutable evidence that they're wrong. We often simply cannot let go of them. These ideas from hell often simply refuse to die, no matter how often struck down. An investment plan built on conventional wisdom is doomed. A successful investment strategy for the 21st century requires a clear understanding of the environment. You must re-examine all of your preconceived notions, abandon the useless, and be willing to incorporate the many useful new advances into your strategy.

To date, Wall Street firms and portfolio managers have put too much emphasis on creating new products connected to specific philosophies and have put very little focus on creating investment processes and tools to deal with the dynamic nature of the markets and the dynamic nature of clients' needs. This has led to a lack of success for most investors.

Passive vs. Active Management

You may assume that taking action is always better than not taking action. However, this may not be the case when it comes to investment management. *Passive investment management* is usually defined as buying and holding index funds within a portfolio. In contrast, *active investment management* is characterized by an attempt to add value or beat a specific index by actively buying and selling securities within a portfolio. A running debate over the merits of active versus passive investment management has colored the investment industry for quite some time.

Many would argue that the expenses and trading costs incurred in active investing make it difficult for even the best portfolio manager to add value to a portfolio. "Determinants of Portfolio Performance," a landmark study by Gary P. Brinson, L. Randolph Hood, and Gilbert Beebower, published in the *Financial Analysts Journal* (July–August 1986), studied investment results of ninety-one large pension funds to determine the factors for differing results over a ten-year period. The study considered four factors as contributors to investment results: asset allocation, individual security selection, market timing, and costs. The results were astounding: 93.6 percent of a pension fund's performance was based solely on asset allocation. Less than 7 percent of the performance was attributable to the other three factors combined.

According to the Brinson study, a portfolio's asset allocation has the greatest impact on its performance. Most active managers are fully invested in stocks almost all the time, so they almost never make an overall asset-allocation decision—their activity is instead focused on buying and selling specific stocks.

In contrast, passive investing is truly more "active" because sector weightings within indexes are constantly changing based on market movements. For example, the technology sector made up about 15 percent of the S&P 500 index's capitalization during the early part of the 1990s. By the end of the technology boom in 2000, the technology sector accounted for more than 35 percent of the index. Those changes in sector weightings affect the volatility and ultimate investment performance of the index. Capitalization-weighted indexes like the S&P 500 always have an increased weighting in whatever sector or industry group has gone up the most. Whatever has increased the most will eventually have the biggest drop in the future.

> **Sector:** A distinct subset of a market whose components share similar characteristics. Stocks are often grouped into different sectors depending on the companies' businesses. Standard & Poor's breaks the market into eleven sectors: utilities, consumer staples, transportation, technology, health care, financial, energy, consumer cyclicals, basic materials, capital goods, and communications services.

In addition, passive investing is "active" because the S&P 500 index (and other indexes) changes individual stocks over time. Almost a thousand new companies have been added to the S&P 500 index from its inception in 1957 until today. Forty-nine new technology stocks were added in the year 2000 alone. In contrast, active style-specific investment managers don't vary from their style. In other words, an active investment manager whose investment style is based on buying large capitalized growth stocks won't buy mid-cap value stocks. Active investment managers' portfolios retain a more consistent structure than those portfolios considered passive—the S&P 500 index and most other equity indexes.

The main difference between traditional active and passive management is the fact that active managers actively attempt to buy and sell individual securities that they think will lead to better performance or to beating their equivalent index. The truth is that asset allocation and sector and industry group weightings have much more impact on returns than individual stock selection if the investment manager holds many stocks. The more individual securities the active investment manager holds, the less impact stock selection has on her ability to outperform an index. For example, what would be the impact on performance from each stock in a portfolio of 100 stocks with each equally weighted at 1 percent of the total portfolio? Very little.

Here's another way to look at it. After kicker Adam Vinatieri joined the Indianapolis Colts, quarterback Peyton Manning asked him to call the coin toss at the beginning of a game. The Colts lost the toss and Manning later said, albeit jokingly, that he wouldn't let Vinatieri call the coin toss again. Clearly, Vinatieri's call had no affect on the coin toss itself. (He picked a random choice, heads or tails, with a 50/50 chance of being right.) Traditional active management is similar to a coin toss. The activity—trading many individual securities like calling the toss—doesn't have a meaningful impact on the result. The problem with active management is that there is a fee for making the call.

The bottom line is that asset allocation has the biggest impact on performance. Both traditional passive and active management require another financial advisor or the individual investor to make the asset allocation decision. Sector and industry weightings for passive management—indexing—are generally determined by current market capitalization. Active managers determine weightings generally based on investment style.

Wall Street prefers active management because activity generates fees and commissions through trading actively managed investment products. Academics tend to prefer passive management because their studies show little if any value added to justify the additional costs beyond indexing.

Both traditional passive and active management philosophies have their flaws. Based on my experience, I favor the traditional passive over the traditional active management approach. Most index funds are truly more diversified than portfolios designed by style-specific active managers. The area where active managers make their active decisions—stock selection—has the least impact on results. If you're going to participate in an active process, then the activity should have a meaningful impact on the outcome. An investor must be convinced that activity is worth the cost and will make a meaningful difference in the pursuit of lifelong performance—and that argument can't be made for traditional active management.

Why Not Just Invest in Index Funds?

Many financial writers suggest that performance results from index funds are better than those from an actively managed portfolio or managed mutual funds. Should you then invest in an index fund like the S&P 500 index? That's a good question. Study after study shows that most investment management styles don't do as well as their equivalent market indexes after expenses. Thus it's hard to make a case for many of the traditional standardized investment processes or products offered by Wall Street firms versus an index fund or portfolio of various index funds.

Index: A statistical measure of change in an economy or a securities market. In the case of financial markets, an index is essentially an imaginary portfolio of securities representing a particular market or a portion of it. Each index has its own calculation methodology and is usually expressed in terms of a change from a base value. Thus, the percentage change is more important than the actual numeric value. For example, knowing that a stock exchange is at, say, 12,000 doesn't tell you much. However, knowing that the index has risen 10 percent over the last year to 12,000 gives a much better demonstration of performance.

Standard & Poor's 500 (S&P 500): Five hundred companies selected by the S&P Index Committee, a team of analysts and economists at Standard and Poor's, for their market size, liquidity, and industry grouping. This list is meant to reflect the risk/return of U.S. large-cap stocks as a whole. Standard and Poor's is a financial services company that rates stocks and corporate and municipal bonds according to risk profiles.

Standard & Poor's 500 index (S&P 500 index): An index consisting of the 500 stocks in the S&P 500. The S&P 500 index is designed to be a leading indicator of U.S. equities. The Dow Jones Industrial Average (DJIA) was at one time the most renowned index for U.S. stocks, but because the DJIA contains only 30 companies, most people agree that the S&P 500 is a better representation of the U.S. market.

Most investment products' fees are high compared to index funds. Unless an investment process or manager can make a value-added case for the added expense of a non-index fund, an investor should choose index funds over most traditional methods of investing. The next question is, "Are index funds the very best way to invest?" To understand the answer to that question, you need to learn a little more about index funds, their expected returns, and their fluctuation. To help explain this concept, we prepared a study of S&P 500 returns from 1926 through 2005—eighty years of data (see figure 8.1).

The average return from 1926 until 2005 has been about 10.4 percent. Because most investors prefer to limit the fluctuation in their portfolio to an acceptable range, the question becomes, "If my average return is 10.4 percent, how many years can I expect the return to be between 8 and 12 percent?" This comfort range would make most people looking for a 10 percent return feel comfortable. But as you can see, only five years out of eighty have had a return between 8 and 12 percent.

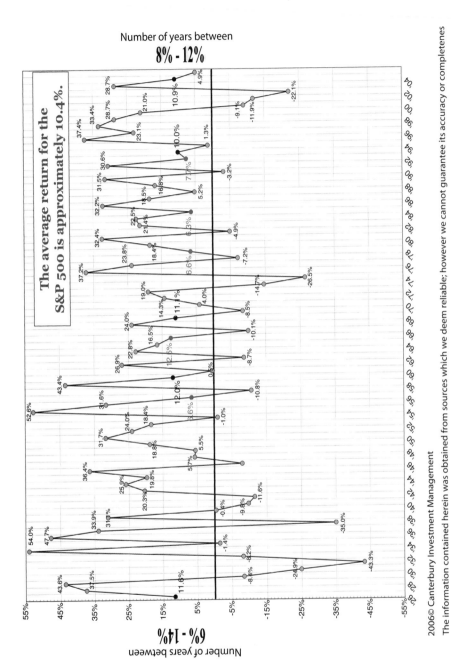

FIGURE 8.1 S&P 500 annual returns 1926–2005

Nasdaq: The world's first electronic stock market. This computerized system facilitates trading and provides price quotations on some 5,000 of the more actively traded over-the-counter stocks. Unlike the New York Stock Exchange and the American Stock Exchange, the Nasdaq doesn't have a physical trading floor that brings buyers and sellers together; all trading is done over a network of computers and telephones.

Dow Jones Industrial Average (DJIA): A price-weighted average of thirty significant stocks traded on the New York Stock Exchange and the Nasdaq. Often referred to as "the Dow," the DJIA is the oldest index in the world.

Index fund: A portfolio of investments that is weighted the same as a stock-exchange index in order to mirror its performance. Investing in an index fund is a form of passive investing. The primary advantage to such a strategy is the lower management expense ratio on an index fund.

What if we widen the comfort range to between 6 and 14 percent? Only ten times in eighty years has the annual return fallen in that zone. That means for seven out of eight years, the return at the end of the year was either below 6 percent or above 14 percent! In his book *Stocks for the Long Run* (McGraw-Hill, 2002), Jeremy Siegel states, "The real return on equities has averaged 7.0 percent [after inflation] per year over the past 195 years. This means that purchasing power has, on average, doubled in the stock market every 10 years. With an inflation of 3 percent per year, a 7.0 percent real return translates into a 10.2 percent average annual money return in equities." An investor in the S&P 500 index would have had to deal with a great deal of fluctuation as well as psychological risk to generate a little more than a 7 percent return after inflation over the long run.

So, what's the answer to the question, "Should I just invest in index funds?" If you're comfortable with returns ranging *below 6 percent or above 14 percent* for seven of eight years, the answer is yes. Sometimes, a wide range of short-term outcomes averages to the intended purpose. Averaging a return of 10.4 percent over eighty years may be acceptable, but earning returns under 6 percent or over 14 percent in seven of eight years may lead to some severe stress! In reality, the answer to the index fund question may be no.

Another Argument Against Index Funds

Efficient market theory states that investors should be rewarded with higher rates of return based on the degree of fluctuation they're required to endure. More fluctuation should justify a higher rate of return. Higher fluctuation also requires more time (years) to yield the average expected return.

The most common measurement of fluctuation for the long-term expected rate of return is called the standard deviation. Figure 8.2 shows the average annual expected returns for one, two, and three standard deviations.

Standard deviation: A statistical measure of the historical volatility of a mutual fund or portfolio.

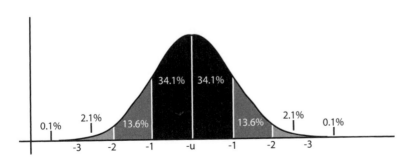

FIGURE 8.2 S&P 500 Index standard deviation

Almost everyone asks, "How much do you think I will earn on my portfolio?" Market cycles are long, but people tend to think in terms of annual returns. Standard deviation is a formula that gives the variation of returns you can expect over one year.

The S&P stock index has averaged a little more than a 10 percent return from 1926 to 2005 with a standard deviation of about 20 percent. What range of returns can you expect over one year? One standard deviation means that you can expect as much as a 30 percent gain (10 percent plus the standard deviation of 20 percent) in a good year, or as much as a 10 percent loss (10 percent minus the standard deviation of 20 percent) in a bad year. That means you can expect the upward range to be about a 30 percent gain and the lower range to be a 10 percent loss for 68.27 percent of the time!

What about the rest of the time? If we use two standard deviations, we have 95.45 percent probability of capturing the high to low expected return for one year. By taking the 10 percent average expected return for the stock market, you can expect a one-year range in return from a 50 percent gain (10 percent plus 20 percent plus 20 percent) to a 30 percent loss (10 percent minus 20 percent minus 20 percent) about 95 percent of the time.

Dealing with potential fluctuations of anywhere from a 50 percent gain to a 30 percent loss is a lot of risk to receive a 10 percent average return. Ask yourself if buying an index fund like the S&P 500 is the best you can do. It's fully subject to this positive 50 percent to negative 30 percent range about 95 percent of the time! And many examples reinforce this concept. For example, the S&P 500 index dropped 50 percent between March 24, 2000 and July 24, 2002, from 1,600 to 800.

This concept of reducing a portfolio's fluctuations within a narrow range is key. You can get a higher return with less risk—but not simply by utilizing index funds.

Shifting Your Thinking

Numerous studies show that past performance has no meaningful bearing on future results and is actually more likely to have a negative impact on the future. In other words, fund managers and mutual funds with a recent past outperformance will generally underperform in the future. Frank Armstrong, the founder of Investor Solutions, Inc., notes in his book *The Informed Investor* (American Management Association, 2003):

A recent study examined mutual fund performance by category over several five-year time periods. Funds were divided into quartiles by past total performance, and then followed for an additional five years. The results were enough to blow your mind! A top quartile fund had just less than a 50% chance of being in the top half during the following five years. A bottom quartile fund had just slightly more than a 50% chance of being in the top half during the following five-year period. In other words, we can't count on either winners or losers to repeat!

Armstrong adds:

Perhaps the most sophisticated publication among the popular business press is Forbes. One would suspect that if picking next year's winner can be done, Forbes would have the resources to do it. They have for years published their "Honor Roll of Mutual Funds." If you had invested steadily in the Forbes funds, you would have had very disappointing results. This underperformance is so consistent and widely known in the industry that many mutual fund wholesale sales representatives consider being so honored the kiss of death.

A disclaimer such as "Past performance is no guarantee of future results" is required on all marketing materials showing performance information. Yet Wall Street continues to use past performance to predict future results. Why do brokerage firms spend so much time focusing on statistically irrelevant returns? The answer is simple: because they sell—and they motivate people to buy products.

In the vast majority of cases, past performance has no statistical significance. For example, the Japanese Nikkei stock market index at the end of 1989 had the best return of all the major developed countries' indexes. Japan's returns were much higher than those obtained in the United States. In fact, Japan's returns for the previous twenty years blew away the United States' returns. But what did the Japanese stock market do after 1989? It basically crashed and burned, and Japan experienced a bear market that lasted for more than fifteen years.

Investors need a fundamental shift in thinking. Stop thinking that fund results can be extrapolated into the future based on the past. You need to think about setting your comfort range and using a process to manage fluctuations. Even twenty years of great returns isn't long enough and not statistically significant to predict where the market will go. With a process that can respond dynamically to the market, you can manage the risk in a portfolio without having to worry on a day-to-day—or even year-to-year—basis, if an individual market index is up or down.

When was the last time you saw a money manager with a thirty-five or forty-year track record using exactly the same stocks and working with the same researchers for that entire time? Doing so would preclude them from integrating any revolutionary investment strategies that have come from the information age. These constantly changing factors result in statistically irrelevant performance returns.

That's not to say that good investment performance isn't important. It's very important, and it's what all portfolio managers strive to produce. The key question to ask is, "Are you interested in obtaining the best short-term performance or the best lifelong performance?" The two possible answers will send an investor not only in different directions, but in opposite directions.

Investment management approaches with the best short-term performance generally are style-specific and lack diversification. Sometimes they're simply lucky enough to have been invested in whatever was "the place to be" at the right time. Short-term performers benefit from sharp upward spikes in performance. Ultimately, the upward spikes will turn downward. These downward spikes kill long-term performance.

Portfolio managers can't control the market. Portfolio managers *can* control their investment processes. It's important that the process makes logical sense and is dynamic enough to have a low probability of failing during difficult periods in the market.

Managing Asset Allocation

As I mentioned earlier, in the "Determinants of Portfolio Performance" study, 93.6 percent of a pension fund's performance was shown to rely only on asset allocation. Less than 7 percent of performance was attributable to the combined impact of individual security selection, market timing, and costs.

Clearly, asset allocation is critical. A common belief among most investment managers and academics is that a portfolio's asset allocation should remain relatively the same over time. They consider changes in asset allocation to be attempts to time the market. Keeping a consistent asset allocation would work if the volatility of the markets was always the same, but the volatility of the markets is constantly changing. A portfolio's asset allocation needs to change to reflect the current situation in the markets—up or down.

Market timing: The process of attempting to predict future market directions, and investing based on those predictions. The goal is to be in the market when it goes up and out when it goes down.

Remember our example of the diversified and nondiversified portfolios from chapter 7? The nondiversified portfolio owned only one market class, such as the S&P 500 index. Several uncorrelated investment classes could reflect the diversified portfolio, such as U.S. stocks, bonds, real estate, international stocks, and cash equivalents. Again, the difference in performance in the two portfolios was a 0 percent return in the nondiversified portfolio and a 12.5 percent return in the diversified portfolio. Not only did the diversified portfolio have a substantially higher return, but it earned its 12.5 percent return with half the risk of the nondiversified portfolio.

The key to portfolio management is having the ability to manage risk. If you can't manage risk, you can't manage the outcome. It's as simple as that. The first step in managing risk is to quantify risk.

Portfolio RiskGrades®

In 1994, J.P. Morgan, the global investment bank, launched RiskMetrics®, an approach to the risk measurement of financial assets. In 1998, RiskMetrics was set up as a separate company with J.P. Morgan and Reuters, the world's largest financial-information provider, as the largest shareholders. RiskMetrics quickly became the standard for institutions worldwide to measure and manage their financial risks. RiskMetrics gave financial managers the ability to quantify the risk of each of their financial investments and to compare it to their expected returns in order to make more informed investment decisions.

The need to measure risk extends beyond institutional investing. Typically, a brokerage or investment house provides an individual investor with detailed return information. However, the best they can do with risk information is to say that "this stock or portfolio is aggressive," which is understood to be riskier than "this stock or portfolio is conservative." Investors know that stocks are riskier than bonds, and bonds are riskier than cash, but until recently, no one knew by how much or how to quantify the total risk of their entire portfolio.

Enter the analysts at RiskMetrics. First they developed risk measurements for institutional investors. They then designed RiskGrades® for individual investors and advisors. RiskGrades provides online analytics that let you measure the risk of stocks, bonds, funds, and portfolios as a whole. All of the RiskGrades components are based on the same RiskMetrics research and technology used by thousands of leading global institutions and regulators.

Utilizing RiskGrades gives you a better understanding of the level of risk and how much a portfolio is benefiting from diversification. RiskMetrics doesn't make, buy, or sell recommendations or predict which stocks will perform better in any one year. However, RiskGrades provides information about risk so you or your portfolio manager can determine the best investments for your portfolio.

RiskGrades is scaled from zero to values over 1,000 for individual securities, where 100 corresponds to the average RiskGrade of an index of international equities during normal market conditions. RiskGrades change over time, such that you could expect the

S&P 500 index to have a RiskGrade of 100 during normal times and of 150 during times of uncertainty or instability (political, economic, and so on).

The following table represents a general range for different asset allocations. The RiskGrade ranges will change based on the overall volatility of the financial markets at any given time.

Risk Grade Scale During Normal Conditions

Risk Grade	5	30–40	40–60	50–80	50–80	60–130+
Asset	T-bills	7–10 year Treasury Notes	"Balanced Conservative" 50% stocks 50% bonds	20–30 year bonds	"Balanced Growth" 70% stocks 30% bonds	Stocks

RiskGrades allows an apples-to-apples comparison of investment risk across all asset classes and regions. Therefore, we can say that a Brazilian stock with a RiskGrade of 300 is six times as risky as an Asian bond fund with a RiskGrade of 50. We aren't limited to single stocks or countries.

The cornerstone of a profitable investment strategy is risk management. We're all taught risk management as children: "Look both ways before crossing the street." Solid risk-management techniques make the return clear but suggest considering risk first. Similarly, financial risk management focuses not only on the use of mathematics, but also on sound commonsense guidelines.

Risk is uncertainty. In investing, risk is typically measured by volatility or variability of returns. For example, the daily variability of returns for the S&P 500 index and Yahoo! stock in 1999 was 1.1 percent and 5.6 percent, respectively. Yahoo!'s returns were five times as risky as those of the S&P 500 index. Yet Yahoo!'s stock outperformed the S&P 500 by 229 percent. Why? Because risk allows for a greater opportunity for a stock to make a higher—as well as a lower—return. Higher volatility means the possibility of larger losses and larger gains.

Investment	1999 daily volatility	1999 return	Biggest 1999 daily drop	Biggest daily return
S&P 500 index	1.1%	19.6%	–3.5%	2.8%
Yahoo! stock	5.6%	248.9%	–23.9%	13.5%

The lesson is this: Rather than avoid risk entirely, the revolutionary investor should avoid taking poorly understood risks and instead choose risks whose potential upside justifies the potential downside—or, better yet, you can learn to benefit from fluctuation. The ability to understand, measure, and manage risk empowers you to make better decisions and profit. Again, technological advances have revolutionized how we measure and manage risk.

With proper diversification, a portfolio can be less risky than its individual components. Not only can you use RiskGrades to calculate the risk of the components of a portfolio, but you can also calculate the risk of the portfolio as a whole. For example, let's look at a portfolio of four well-known stocks:

Stock	RiskGrade
Johnson & Johnson	48
General Electric	57
Microsoft	112
AT&T	82
Portfolio	46

The portfolio's RiskGrade of 46 is less than the RiskGrade of each individual stock. Due to portfolio diversification, the total is less risky than the parts. If we add cash and bonds, this portfolio's RiskGrade goes even lower:

Stock	RiskGrade
Johnson & Johnson	48
General Electric	57
Microsoft	112
AT&T	82
Cash	0
7-10 Year Treasury Bonds	19
Portfolio	27

The Revolution Is Creating New Tools

Another benefit from the Information Age is the fact that many new tools have been created to deal with the dynamic market environment.

Exchange-Traded Funds (ETFs)

There is a revolution within the investment community, and few outside the Wall Street elite are aware of it. If you ask the general public what U.S. investment company has the most assets under management, they might reply with Vanguard, Fidelity, or Schwab. The true answer is Barclays Global Investors, the industry leader in exchange-traded funds (ETFs).

ETFs have exploded in popularity. That's because large institutional investors understand the important role they can play in a portfolio. Outside of Wall Street, however, few people know what they are. That is changing. In time, ETFs will be as commonly known as mutual funds.

ETFs were introduced in the United States in 1993 with the advent of the Standard & Poor's Depository Receipt, commonly known as S&P 500 Spyder (SPY). The Nasdaq 100 Tracking Stock (QQQQ) gained popularity in 1999, but ETFs' real growth began in 2000 when Barclays introduced the iShares ETF family. Today there are many ETF choices, and combined assets in ETFs are around $356 billion.

Exchange-traded fund: A security that tracks an index, a commodity, or a basket of assets like an index fund, but trades like a stock on an exchange, thus experiencing price changes throughout the day as it's bought and sold. Such a fund provides the diversification of an index fund as well as the ability to sell short, buy on margin, and purchase as little as one share. Another advantage is that the expense ratios for most ETFs are lower than those of the average mutual fund. Buying and selling ETFs results in the same trading costs as with any security.

ETFs are like index funds, but they're traded throughout the day just like stocks. Similar to index mutual funds, most ETFs represent ownership in an underlying portfolio of securities that tracks a specific market index. That index may cover an entire market or slices of the market broken down by capitalization, sector, style, country, and so on. Exchange-traded products that track currencies and commodities are also being introduced. Savvy investors or portfolio managers can buy an entire market segment, or an international market, with one trade.

Portfolio volatility is easily reduced by owning ETFs that have low correlations to one another. Portfolio volatility can also be managed using the innovative technique of allocating funds to an inverse ETF (an ETF that moves opposite to overall market movement).

Inverse/Reverse Funds

The market doesn't always go up. One tool investors can use in such an environment is a reverse or inverse fund. These funds hold securities that go in the opposite direction of their equivalent market index—for example, the S&P 500. These new securities were created by companies like Rydex Investments and ProFunds. They're now available in the form of ETFs. They can be used to lower volatility during highly volatile times. Inverse funds can also be used to make money when the market goes down; when the market goes down, inverse funds go up. For example, an inverse S&P 500 fund seeks to provide investment returns that inversely correlate to the daily performance of the S&P 500 index. Inverse funds create a possibility for the portfolio manager to benefit from declines in the market.

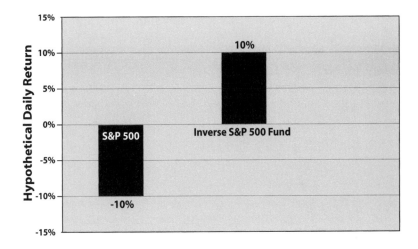

FIGURE 8.3 Inverse fund

Setting Your Portfolio Thermostat™

A first and critical step in managing fluctuations in your portfolio has to do with setting your comfort range. When fluctuations get too high, most people begin to feel a little anxious. When fluctuations are too low, nothing is happening, the market gets boring, and it's hard to make money.

Remember the crew of the S.S. Minnow, who were trapped as castaways on Gilligan's Island? They set out for a three-hour tour and were stuck in the clothes they left home in. Although Ginger always had on a new slinky dress and the Howells seemed to have luggage, Mary Ann, the Professor, the Skipper, and Gilligan seemed pretty comfortable year-round in their island attire. Growing up in Midwestern winters, the shipwrecked life of *Gilligan's Island* seemed relatively appealing.

Have you ever wondered why the castaways always seemed so comfortable? A quick analysis of the average change in temperature on Gilligan's Island (actually Coconut Island, Hawaii) shows that temperatures generally ranged from 70 to 80 degrees—hardly a bitter climate by any standard. Compare that to a similar analysis of the temperature fluctuations in my hometown of Indianapolis, Indiana.

As you can see in figure 8.4, temperatures are volatile in Indiana, ranging from sweltering heat in July to frostbite cold in February.

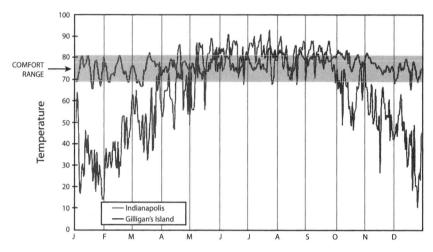

FIGURE 8.4 Temperature chart

If you think about how a thermostat manages temperature fluctuations, then you know you can set the highs and lows to your personal comfort range, usually similar to the comfortable climes of Coconut Island. Too hot? The air conditioner comes on. Too cold? The furnace kicks in.

In the same way, you have probably experienced market fluctuations that pushed you outside your personal comfort range. You may have felt the sting of a volatile market's sunburn and the chill of an idle market's frost, if you will. For example, markets were very volatile (too hot) in April 2003. You may remember when the Iraqis had a rope around the neck of Saddam Hussein's statue and were pulling it to the ground. It seemed as though the closer the statue got to the ground, the more the market dropped. The temperature of the market at that time, measured by RiskGrades, was about 120 degrees (very hot).

At other times, market temperatures haven't been so prone to fluctuations. In 2005 and 2006, the fluctuations were too low; looking at your portfolio was like watching paint dry. The volatility index, or the temperature, of the stock market then was too cold—about 50 degrees, which signified low volatility.

Volatility: The relative rate at which the price of a stock or security moves up and down. If the price of a stock moves up and down rapidly over short time periods, it has high volatility. If the price almost never changes, it has low volatility.

Why is managing fluctuation within a comfort range important for them? As you saw with the two portfolios starting at $100, portfolio B—the more diversified of the two—had half the fluctuation and made more money. More often than not, aggressive investing doesn't yield higher returns. Being aggressive means you're shooting for a higher rate of return in a short period of time. By definition, an aggressive investor lacks diversification; therefore, that investor wouldn't receive the benefits of diversification.

If a sharp decline causes your portfolio to lose 50 to 60 percent of your investment, it's difficult to get that money back. Proper diversification and a process for managing price fluctuation, as a means to enhance return and keep fluctuation in a narrow range, will optimize your portfolio return and make you less subject to psychological risk. It can also help optimize your portfolio's return. You'll get a higher rate of return with less fluctuation and less psychological risk—it's the best of all worlds.

The goal of a revolutionary investment process is to manage fluctuation within the investor's comfort range and to make market fluctuations benefit the investor. To help shift investors' thoughts away from worrying about short-term performance and to help them understand how to benefit from a fluctuating market, I use the Portfolio Thermostat™, a technique for keeping the level of fluctuation within the investors' stated comfort range. Consider the Portfolio Thermostat an alternate approach to sitting back and observing the changing volatility in financial markets.

The following table shows how the Portfolio Thermostat works. In the first example, from 2002, the market temperature was 150 degrees (high volatility). In the second example, the market temperature dropped to only 50 degrees (low volatility). In other words, the stock market was three times more volatile in the first example than in the second. That means an investor whose assets were in 33 percent stocks and 67 percent cash (portfolio X) when the temperature was 150 degrees had the same volatility as an investor with 100 percent stocks (portfolio Y) when the volatility in the market was 50 degrees.

The critical point is that changing the investor's asset allocation is the only way to address market risk changes.

The goal of the Portfolio Thermostat is to maintain the fluctuation in a portfolio within a narrow and predictable range. In April 2002, the S&P 500 volatility index reached a level of about 150, but the portfolio volatility goal was 50. Because stocks had a risk of 150 at that time and cash always has a volatility of zero, we would put 33 percent of our money in the S&P 500 index fund and 67 percent in cash to achieve the portfolio volatility goal of 50.

In December 2006, the volatility of the S&P 500 had dramatically declined to only 50. Because our goal is to maintain the portfolio's risk at 50, we would need 100 percent stocks and 0 percent cash (portfolio Y) to keep the risk at 50.

Let's look at one last example. Suppose the volatility of the stock market rises to 100. We need to reduce the risk of 100 percent stocks by half to meet our goal, which means that 50 percent of our money is in the S&P 500 index and 50 percent is in cash (portfolio Z).

In all three situations, the Portfolio Thermostat adjusts the heat on the portfolio to give it a better chance of obtaining a reasonable return without creating excessive fluctuation. These temperature changes give the investor a chance to see some real gains.

Before we had a controlled technique for managing fluctuation, the traditional belief was that we should keep the portfolio's asset allocation the same all the time. That strategy would work if the volatility of the markets was always the same, but it's not. The temperature, or volatility, of the market is always changing from hot (high fluctuations) to cold (low fluctuations). The Portfolio Thermostat changes asset allocation over time to offset fluctuation. When the stock market is volatile, the thermostat reduces a portfolio's exposure to stocks. When the stock market is less volatile, the thermostat tells the portfolio manager to increase stock exposure. The goal is to keep the portfolio within a consistent volatility range as opposed to keeping a consistent asset allocation.

	S&P 500 volatility index	Portfolio	Asset allocation	Calculation	Portfolio volatility	Portfolio volatility goal
April 2002	150	X	33% stocks, 67% cash	(33% x 150) + (67% x 0)	50	50
	150	Y	100% stocks, 0% cash	100% x 150	150	50
December 2006	50	X	33% stocks, 67% cash	(33% x 50) + (67% x 0)	16.5	50
	50	Y	100% stocks, 0% cash	100% x 50	50	50
Future	100	Z	50% stocks, 50% cash	(50% x 100) + (50% x 0)	50	50

Techniques for managing fluctuation within a comfort range are new developments in portfolio management, and the old models don't address such issues. As a result, you may have experienced erratic fluctuations and returns over the last few years. The investor revolution will help individuals see a greater consistency in their returns, paving the way to greater lifelong performance.

If the cast of *Gilligan's Island* moved to the Midwest, they'd be uncomfortable when the temperature dipped below 50 degrees. But if we put Ginger in a fur coat, she'd probably be more comfortable. On the other hand, she wouldn't fare well in the dog days of August wrapped in designer mink; she'd want her bikini. Similarly, you need the ability to "change clothes" (or securities) in a portfolio based on the seasons. You need to hold more defensive and less volatile stocks when the market is hot, and to hold more growth-oriented stocks that inherently have a little more fluctuation when the market becomes cold.

To remain comfortable in all seasons, those of us who don't live on Coconut Island understand that we need both a furnace and an air conditioner, connected to a thermostat and adjusted to our comfort range. If your goal is to remain comfortable in a changing market climate, you must equip your portfolio with a thermostat that assesses market conditions (primarily risk) and takes steps to adjust the portfolio.

New Tools and the Thermostat

The Portfolio Thermostat uses techniques to reduce the risk in your portfolio. It can also be used to design asset allocation—the percentages of stocks, bonds, and cash your portfolio needs. The thermostat allows investors and portfolio managers alike to see that further diversification of a portfolio is needed in order to maintain your comfort zone. The ultimate goal of the Portfolio Thermostat is to keep the level of risk within your comfort range, but it can also reduce stresses associated with picking investments, which leads to an even greater sense of comfort and confidence in your future investment choices. The Portfolio Thermostat is a tool that fits into the dynamic process to manage many concepts we've discussed, and to make those aspects of a market work for you.

How do you know the volatility in the market at a given time?

In figure 8.5, the dashed line represents the change in the volatility index (as measured by the RiskGrade) over the last four years. Remember, the volatility index doesn't reflect whether the market is up or down; it simply reflects the change in volatility. As you can see, the volatility in the S&P 500 changed from a maximum of 181 to a minimum of 44—a change of more than 400 percent. The band in the middle is an example of a volatility index or investor comfort range of 60 to 80. There were only a few times when the volatility of the S&P 500 was in the investor comfort range. Most of the time, the volatility was either higher or lower than this investor wanted.

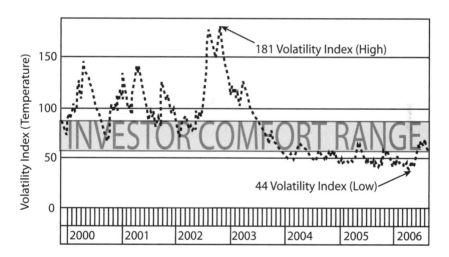

FIGURE 8.5 S&P 500 market volatility

The traditional way of reducing the volatility range is to diversify the portfolio by combining different market classes, such as putting stocks and bonds together in the same portfolio. Figure 8.6 shows a portfolio invested 60 percent in an S&P 500 index fund and 40 percent in seven- to ten-year treasury notes. A 60/40 stock/bond

asset allocation would be considered conservative by most investment experts. As you can see, the volatility index fluctuated from a
high of 107 to a low of 28. Remember, the investor comfort range
is customized to meet the investor's personal needs. In this example,
the desired comfort range was 60 to 80. There were periods where
the 60/40 blend was too volatile, and there were times when it was
not volatile enough.

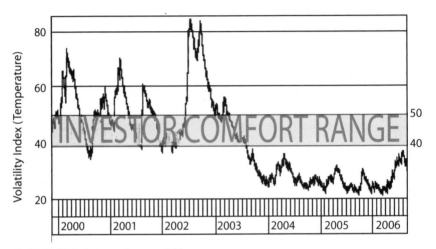

FIGURE 8.6 Sample portfolio

One goal of the revolutionary investment process is to maintain
the portfolio's fluctuation within a specified comfort range. Because
it's an undeniable truth that markets fluctuate and those fluctuations vary over time, a consistent asset allocation will cause a high
variability in a portfolio's risk level. Using the Portfolio Thermostat,
investors can designate their own personal comfort range in terms
of volatility or fluctuation. A major tool in executing the Portfolio
Thermostat technique is changing asset allocation to reflect the
changes in market fluctuation at a given time. In addition, reverse
funds can be used to "turn up" or "turn down" the thermostat as
market conditions warrant. The goal is to keep the investor's portfolio in his or her specific comfort range, shown in figure 8.7 by the
dots in the comfort range band.

FIGURE 8.7 Fluctuations inside the comfort range

Don't Confuse Companies with Stocks

Historically, portfolio managers have used fundamental analysis—the study of companies—to pick stocks. However, most analysts who say they can identify a stock or group of stocks by using fundamental analysis are also the first to admit they have trouble with timing, or knowing when to buy and when to sell. They will take a stance that a particular stock or industry will out-perform over a period of time, but knowing exactly when to buy and when to sell isn't something most claim to be able to predict.

Fundamental analysis: A method of analyzing a security by using financial, economic, quantitative, and qualitative indicators to determine the intrinsic value. Fundamental analysts study everything that can impact the security's value, from macroeconomic factors (such as the overall economy and industry conditions) to individually specific factors (such as the financial condition and management of companies).

Fundamental analysis focuses on the company—the competition, its management, the product the company produces, and its financial statements—as well as other company-specific information. This type of analysis allows people to buy a stock because they "like" a company. Just because a company is a "good company" doesn't always mean that its stock will outperform.

Fundamental analysis is based on the theory that a mispricing in the marketplace may occur that can be exploited by evaluating a company's fundamentals. Further, fundamental analysis is based on the theory that analysts can consistently uncover fundamental information that the market hasn't already reflected in the current price of the stock. Fundamental analysis is focused more on the company and less on the stock.

The hallmark of fundamental analysis lies in analyzing information in a way that uncovers market inefficiencies that result in mispricing a security. With the growth of the Internet, an enormous amount of information is freely available about almost any publicly traded company. Much of it can be found by anyone who visits Web sites maintained by the company, by brokerage houses, or by other research operations. Fundamental research conveys much less (if any) meaningful advantage to today's investor because everyone is looking at the same information at the same time. Widespread access to information as a result of the communications and Information Age has made the market more efficient: It's difficult to uncover information or knowledge that the market doesn't already know.

Many academics believe that you can't add value by doing fundamental research. They state that the markets are so efficient in the pricing of securities that choosing stocks based on fundamental research is no more profitable than randomly picking stocks without knowing anything about the company or stock. Hence, I am (and you should be) intensely interested in revolutionary approaches to security selection that may have a better chance of adding value than the more traditional methods.

Technical analysis is the study of the supply and demand or accumulation and distribution of securities. This discipline has become more popular and effective due to the same advances in information technology that have lessened the effectiveness of fundamental analysis. Being able to determine when to buy and when to sell, in order to participate in the period when a security is performing at its best, is critical. Having a good sell discipline is even more important than a good buy discipline: You have to know when to get out. If you wait until some fundamental news indicates that the company has a problem, it's too late.

> **Technical analysis:** A method of evaluating securities by analyzing statistics generated by market activity, such as past prices and volume. Technical analysts don't attempt to measure a security's intrinsic value, but instead use charts and other tools to identify patterns that can suggest future activity.

Brad Herndon, a portfolio manager and securities analyst, who holds both Chartered Market Technician (CMT) and Chartered Financial Analyst® (CFA®) certifications, states:

> *Currently, more fundamental portfolio managers are recognizing the benefits of technical analysis to enhance investment returns and manage risk. Technical analysis enables portfolio managers and analysts to quickly assimilate a broad array of factors that may impact their buy or sell decisions. In fact, the ability to compile data and analyze technical indicators has been enhanced by computer technology and improved access to information. Moreover, because the global capital markets consist of many buyers and sellers, technical analysis provides a method to assess the supply and demand for a security, and a means to analyze the sentiment or motivation of the buyers and sellers.*

If you're interested in stocks, bonds, and the direction of the market, it makes much more sense to study stocks, bonds, and the market than it does to study companies. If you're interested in buying a company, then study the company. Make sure you're buying a good company, but don't confuse it with the stock. Companies and stocks are entirely different things.

Navigating Changing Markets

The market changes direction abruptly—rising or falling rapidly—when most people least expect it. How can you weather market downturns with minimum damage? How can you know when a stock is going out of favor so you can remove it from your portfolio? Conversely, how can you know when a stock is poised for a big increase in value, so you can increase your stake in it?

Of course, the short answer is, you can never be sure. However, you can use indicators of supply and demand to improve the probability of predicting the direction a stock is headed. The law of supply and demand is the foundation of technical analysis.

Technical analysis can often help you know the probability of when a stock should be sold (as it begins to lose value) or when a stock is about to increase greatly in value. Such information can help you position your portfolio to weather or even profit from rapidly changing markets. Technical analysis tries to predict a stock's rise or fall not based on prior performance but rather based on economic and market conditions surrounding the stock.

Another advantage of technical analysis is that it allows you to look at all tradable markets and securities—domestic and foreign—in the same way. The indicators work the same whether the stock is IBM, Daimler Chrysler, the Dow Jones Industrial Average, or the Japanese Nikkei index. Variables such as country of origin, industry sector, political stability of the country, and currency fluctuations all contribute to and are reflected in the technical indicators.

Unlike fundamental analysis, which is based on theories, technical analysis is based on a law: the law of supply and demand. The law of supply and demand of stocks (and, thus, the movement of markets) is directly related to human emotions. The only way a stock can go up in value is for more people to initiate buys than sells. Stocks can go down only if more people initiate sells than buys. If many people think the price of a stock will rise, they buy the stock, and their demand drives up the price. On the other hand, if many people think a stock isn't performing well, they sell it and drive its price down. In a nutshell, technical analysis can help portfolio managers choose stocks by analyzing the price action of a security or the market.

The Information Age has helped to create a revolution in technical analysis. We now have more relevant trading data and the computer firepower to analyze it. Not so long ago, it would have taken a roomful of engineers with handheld calculators to crunch numbers that some expert systems or artificial intelligence–based programs can now produce in seconds. Technical-analysis programs can combine data on the daily price and sales volume of a stock into hundreds of rules and indicators. By analyzing fifty to sixty of these indicators simultaneously, expert system software can generate a buy or sell recommendation for a particular stock.

Fundamental analysis tends to be more black and white. You're either right or wrong. For example, many fundamental analysts had buy recommendations on Enron beginning at 80 and even as the stock dropped to 70, 60, and lower. Most kept their buy ratings because they had no fundamental information to make them believe their original analysis had changed. If Enron was a good value at 80, then it was even better at 70, 60, or lower. Eventually, everyone learned the truth about Enron—from the news media. Only then did fundamental analysts lower their ratings based on the new information. The fundamental analysts' opinions on Enron were wrong because they were based on incorrect information. As the stock went down, most analysts became more committed to their opinions because the stock was getting cheaper or selling for a better value. It was a recipe for disaster.

Technical analysis is based on the probabilities of stocks behaving in a certain way. The probabilities change over time. I owned Enron stock in my managed portfolios but sold the stock when it was just below 70 because it was going down. Most of my technical indicators showed the probabilities were that the stock would continue to decline. I didn't know why—we all learned the reason later. What I did know was that the probabilities had changed for the worse, and it was time to sell. Basing decision-making on probabilities makes the analyst less emotional. It's much easier to cut losses when a security or the market begins to move south. I've found that such systems greatly enhance technical analysts' abilities to accurately predict the future movement of a stock price, as well as the market as a whole.

Investment Policy Statements

As we shift our thinking beyond picking funds or investments based on performance, we start to focus on fluctuation and risk. Remember, overall the markets trend up over time, and fluctuations can be managed if you establish a comfort range. One way to begin the portfolio design process is with the Investment Policy Statement (IPS).

The IPS outlines the investment guidelines and procedures agreed on by the investor that are to be followed by the portfolio manager. The IPS is instrumental in establishing communication and mutual understanding between the investor and the portfolio manager. It's an important tool for avoiding the pitfalls of psychological risk and staying disciplined with investing.

An IPS is an important part of the process of keeping your portfolio's fluctuation within a comfort range, or acceptable level of risk tolerance. Some investors understand the long-term nature of markets; they say they aren't bothered by fluctuation and therefore have no psychological risk.

A well-written IPS increases the likelihood that your portfolio will continue to meet your financial needs. It clarifies the appropriate investment process so you and your portfolio manager know you're on the same page. It identifies your needs, goals, objectives, and risk tolerances, and it establishes reasonable expectations, objectives, and guidelines for investing the portfolio's assets. It defines the responsibilities of investor and portfolio manager, and it encourages effective communication between the two. Perhaps most important, the IPS clarifies the relationship between your money and the freedom to do what you want.

Your IPS should include the following components:

- *Personal financial objectives:* A written paragraph or two about your vision for your money. What's important about the money to you? What's the purpose? How can it be used to bring about rewarding and fulfilling opportunities?

- *Risk guidelines:* These quantify the level of risk you're comfortable with (your comfort range). Discuss with your portfolio manager how she quantifies risk. This component should be more quantifiable than just "aggressive" or "risk-adverse."

- *Asset allocation guidelines:* Asset allocation refers to your portfolio's blend of stocks, bonds, and cash equivalents. Finding the best asset mix is crucial if you want to meet your goals. A balanced portfolio has an appropriate mix of stocks, bonds, and cash equivalents at all times and is designed to meet the agreed-upon risk targets. Your asset allocation should change over time based on market fluctuation and outlook. The goal is to adjust the asset allocation in a way to keep the fluctuations in the portfolio within a predictable comfort range.

- *Diversification guidelines:* Your portfolio manager should have a process to help measure the percentage benefit of diversification, and a method to identify your portfolio's volatility.

- *Tax considerations:* Are there any special tax considerations for your portfolio? For example, do you have low-cost-basis stocks or a large tax loss to carry forward? For taxable portfolios, the manager should focus on harvesting short-term tax losses and pursuing long-term capital gains.

An IPS puts your investment strategy in writing and shows the disciplined investment plan upon which you and your portfolio manager agree. You can succeed even if your financial goals are very individually targeted. My years of experience indicate that the best portfolio management style is based on these few rules:

1. *Understand the process of measuring risk in a portfolio.* If you can't manage risk, then you can't manage the outcome. The first step in managing risk is quantifying the risk in the portfolio at any given time.

2. *Learn what proper diversification really means,* and remember that volatility and correlations among securities change over time and in different market environments. As a result, the securities within the portfolio must be managed to reflect the current environment.

3. *Markets are driven by the irrefutable law of supply and demand.* Supply and demand are driven by human emotions. People are most optimistic at the top and most pessimistic at the bottom. Your investment process should be free of emotions.

4. *Portfolios should be managed by using a well-thought-out and tested rules-based system.* Then, there needs to be a dynamic process to adapt the rules and to manage the tools through changing market environments.

Once you understand the rules and the process, you'll be able to choose a portfolio manager who uses them with confidence. You'll be secure in the knowledge that you and/or your portfolio manager are doing everything possible to bring you financial security, regardless of what the market, other investors, and other financial advisors may do.

If you follow the rules-based diversification system described in this chapter, you'll find that time can eliminate the risks of changing your asset allocation. Even if you sell an asset at a loss, time will compensate for the loss. Remember, the value of your portfolio today is no more relevant than its value two years ago or its value two years from now. The only time your portfolio's value is relevant is when the entire portfolio is liquidated, which we hope won't happen in our lifetime!

What *will* happen in your lifetime, however, is a greater sense of fulfillment and purpose if you use the concepts and techniques outlined in this chapter to help support your personal vision of who you want to become. Utilizing the proper investment tools and process in a dynamic market environment to create a customized investment portfolio is the key. Money isn't the most important thing in life, but it's a vital instrument that gives you the freedom to become who you want to be and to do the things you've always wanted to do. Having an investment process designed for successful lifelong performance keeps you more focused on what really matters: having the time of your life.

Chapter 9

The Investor Revolution
Is Now

"A revolution is an idea which has found its bayonets."

—Napoleon Bonaparte

In a historical context, revolutionaries are by no means a new breed. They were here long before the boomer generation appeared and will be around long after. They have evolved throughout the ages and are the trailblazers who set forth to change the world for younger generations.

Looking back across history, we see that true success stories involve those individuals who found a revolutionary process for dealing with their dynamic environments, riding it to great renown, and sticking with the process to reap its fruits. Wall Street is no exception. Its history is peppered with revolutionaries who took advantage of investment opportunities and developed processes that worked famously. As far back as the late 1800s, to as recently as the infamous year of 1929, there were any number of Wall Street titans whose financial successes awe investment industry leaders to this day. These stock traders—people like Jacob Little, Jesse Livermore, Jim Fisk, Daniel Drew, and many others—made millions upon millions when a single million, to most investors, seemed an insurmountable goal. The names of these stock and commodity trading revolutionaries still echo among Wall Street historians.

Sadly, a common, dubious thread binds together many success-ful revolutionaries of early Wall Street: Most ended their lives pen-niless, downtrodden, and, in some cases, living in the insane asylum. They rose to greatness but ultimately failed. The reasons underlying their downfall differ very little. With few exceptions, these men had a technique that worked well in certain environments but ultimately failed in others. Jesse Livermore, for example, was a renowned mar-ket technician still commonly noted as one of the greatest stock traders in the history of Wall Street. His legendary mind for num-bers is still revered by the trading community; but, as was the case for many of his contemporaries, his system eventually ran into an environment he didn't expect and thus failed. Livermore's approach didn't manage for risk as well as it managed for profit.

Ironically, the initial Wall Street revolutionaries failed in the long run because they were so successful during certain types of market environments but not all. They speculated marvelously, assigned themselves to big positions within firms, and used leverage to buy securities. Unfortunately, they relied too heavily on processes that worked in the past but couldn't adapt to the changing environ-ment. In other words, their processes were home-run investment strategies that created much excitement as the returns gushed in, but these approaches were successful only for short-term periods. They made a lot of money over a short period of time, but in the end they were penniless. Were they really unlike the investors in the Internet boom of the late 1990s?

Even though these Wall Street legends made millions, most were not successful investors. They never capitalized on their wealth to build any sort of livelihoods that would endure. In a sense, they were like blackjack players who count cards. A great card counter can win 70 of 100 hands and still go broke behind a bad betting system. In Livermore's case, especially, he was a great stock picker, but his money-management system was lacking—a trend that carries over to Wall Street today. Being a good stock picker and a lousy portfolio manager will put you in a position to lose all your money.

Many early Wall Street heavyweights did very well, for a time. The problem was that they relied on tools that worked in the past but couldn't adapt to a dynamic, changing market environment. Throughout its centuries-old history, the stock market has been dynamic and constantly changing—almost always one step ahead of Wall Street investment strategies. When you're dealing with a dynamic market, you need a series of tools and a process that can adapt to different types of market environments. The titans were revolutionaries in manipulating the stock market and cornering other markets. But their Achilles heel was exposed by the certainties of fluctuation and time. Their tricks were limited and ultimately led to their downfall.

Investors who are leading the revolution don't want to follow the footsteps of their predecessors; they want to blaze a new trail that takes advantage of new technologies and processes. Today's investors want to change their Wall Street experience for themselves, but they know there are no real shortcuts. There is no magic number, no golden ticket toward prosperity for the ages. You can learn from the pitfalls of Wall Street, or you can ignore them. The choice is yours. The first important step to successful lifelong investing isn't blowing up in the short term. By avoiding a flawed and static system that keeps all your eggs in one basket, you won't take the big hits to your investment principal that crippled the short-term focused investors of yore. Shortcuts to riches never existed. Chasing the shortcut is a fast track to dying broke. As a new revolutionary, you can do better: By customizing the revolution to fit your life, harnessing information to produce the right answers, and preparing yourself with a dynamic rules-based process, you can achieve lifelong success.

Customize the Revolution to Fit Your Life

The message of the investor revolution is that you must apply the right tools to today's dynamic environments. Unlike traditional approaches, your process has to be flexible. You need realistic expectations for your investments, and you need to plan for your life. Many investors have difficulty specifying exactly what they want; one way to jump that hurdle is to first decide what you *don't* want. Without exception, nobody wants to die broke. A coaching process helps you avoid that fate.

There are tons of investment choices available today but few dynamic processes for managing the choices to meet varying conditions. The traditional, static, assembly-line approach to investing hasn't done well at all. That's a standardized approach to dealing with a dynamic and customized set of circumstances. It's nothing that should intrigue a revolutionary investor.

As chapter 5 showed, the due diligence you take on as an investor should be focused not on finding the right products, but on finding the right expert. With automobiles, you know that your choices in finding the right car are nearly unlimited. Plenty of cars exist that can do the job of transporting you from point A to B, but finding the right car to meet your needs perfectly in all seasons is virtually impossible. Given that, you do the best you can to find the happy medium.

Me, I'm a big car kind of guy. I prefer a large, four-door sedan because it fits most of my needs. On road trips, my car is a veritable couch on wheels. I like the smooth ride. But sometimes my sedan isn't the right car for the job—there's just no way around it.

In the winter, I'm constantly fearful of driving on snow and often wish I'd chosen an SUV as my primary vehicle. In other instances, when I need to shoot downtown and squeeze into a tight parking space, something like a Mini Cooper would be preferable to a beefier sedan. For cruising purposes in the summertime, I find myself wishing I could peel the top down, as I could with a convertible. There are all types of cars, each designed to meet a specific kind of need or environment. I live in a dynamic environment with serious fluctuations in temperature. Unfortunately, like most people, I don't have the option to pick and choose a vehicle of the day to match the weather.

Ideally, as outlandish as this might sound, I'd like to walk to my garage in the morning with a dynamic process to manage cars to my changing driving environment. I'd like to flip a switch and electronically unveil a sort of car carousel. As a revolutionary, I've often envisioned this carousel mechanism and how it could change my driving life. If I had to drive to Louisville, for instance, I'd punch the road car button, and a Mercedes S Class would be at my disposal. A nice day? One button, and there's the convertible Porsche. Snow? No problem—I have my SUV. Operating my car carousel, I'd have an unlimited number of choices to suit whatever the environment called for, and the carousel process could integrate an unlimited number of tools to match my needs with a vehicle.

In many ways, a singular investment process that could handle all market environments is equally far-fetched. Like car dealerships, brokerage firms aren't equipped to cover all elements of a dynamic market. The processes I've outlined in the previous two chapters, such as the Portfolio Thermostat, are equipped to weather and adapt to the environment better than anything else. The objective of personal wealth management is to customize your life goals toward fulfillment—a Sunday afternoon pleasure cruise, if you will—like no generation has ever known before.

The standardized model is meant for only one season, whereas the customized approach deals with multiple uses in all types of weather. Having the wrong automobile for a specific need isn't a life-or-death issue. Having the wrong combination of investments at the wrong time can be hazardous to your wealth.

What I'm championing isn't quite the end-all super carousel of my ideal garage, but it's as close as the investment world can currently get. I hope that reading this book has given you the inspiration and insight to realize that you can customize this revolutionary process to fit your life and your goals.

Harness the Information to Produce the Right Answer

Until a few years ago, I thought a google meant the biggest number that ever existed, as in "That house must've cost google dollars," because that's the only time I'd ever heard the word. Now I know better—and, like millions of Internet surfers around the world, I've come to rely on Google for quick, detailed answers to questions.

> **Google:** A well-known Web search engine that indexes billions of Web pages and provides a free service that searches this index in less than a second.
>
> **Googol:** A number that is equal to 1 followed by 100 zeros, or 10^{100}.

As a revolutionary investor, you have access to the great benefits that the Information Age allows. Today's technology makes information available that can create knowledge, strengthen your business and your life, and offer you a better way to deal with markets. Most investors don't have nearly the successes they should have, because they're still attached to the products of yesteryear. A googol of tools can be used to deal with any type of market environment, but the weakness lies in finding a process to manage those tools.

In 2003, I interviewed my friend and fellow author the late Joseph C. Farah, and he concluded rather humorously that there is no cure for the malady of information anxiety, a common diagnosis in the information age. Farah posited that all forms of media—digital television, newspapers, books, computers, e-mail, journals, virtual reality, the Internet, and so forth—present the ordinary twenty-first-century human being with an overwhelming amount of information. Navigating this information can prove to be a taxing experience. "It has been said that we Americans live in 'an information-rich but knowledge-poor society,' meaning we can't utilize the vast quantities of information available to us and assimilate what information we need as knowledge," wrote Farah. "If we can't turn information we have into knowledge...then we are headlong on a path toward information anxiety."

Farah suggested that, to transform an influx of information and ideas into bona fide knowledge, you must first ask questions of yourself. Namely, you must figure out how much information you really need. "For some, acquiring knowledge and learning is a lifelong, insatiable quest for its own sake. For others, it's a boring chore, a 'death march' of the brain with no visible destination on the horizon."

The reasons behind information overload are obvious, according to Farah. He cited work by author Richard Saul Wurman, who found that a regular weekday edition of *The New York Times* contains more information than the average seventeenth-century Englishman came across in a lifetime. More new information, notes Wurman, has been produced in the last half century than in the previous 5,000 years, and roughly 1,000 books are published every day worldwide. That's a serious amount of information, much more than anyone could hope to digest. Using the Information Age tools now at your fingertips, you have a better chance than ever at cutting through the information waves to find the knowledge you truly need.

> **Information anxiety**: Disquiet "produced by the ever-widening gap between what we understand and what we think we should understand. It's the black hole between data and knowledge, and it happens when information doesn't tell us what we want to or need to know." —Richard Saul Wurman

As a revolutionary driving this new way of thinking about investing, you have to stay hungry for knowledge that will impact your life for the better. Streamline your channels of information to those that feed your idyllic visions of the future. Almost all life transitions involve money and personal finance, and you need to *know* where your best options reside. It's more important than ever to make the connection between your life and your investments; the information is out there to bridge your life with good financial decisions, and it's only a matter of wading through the nonsense to find it.

Revolutionaries Come Prepared

Just as the great bulk of information causes apprehension, many people today consider the area of finances an anxiety-producing topic. They're afraid they're going to get bad advice. They're worried they'll outlive their money. The solution can be found in the emerging field of personal wealth management.

With personal wealth management, you see a functional, win-win relationship between investors and their advisors. Personal wealth managers focus on helping people create a compelling vision of their future lives and integrating customized portfolio management and personal finance through good coaching and education. A personal wealth manager is someone who understands the client's life, dreams, and goals.

This emerging business model, which encourages a client-centered, rather than a sales-centered, relationship, will be a major breakthrough for the financial services industry. Although personal wealth management is in the early, innovative stages of its S-curve, I'm confident that revolutionary investors will demand and ultimately receive the service they deserve.

With personal wealth coaching as part of a personal wealth management strategy, investors are coached through the process by a caring, competent advisor and can begin to develop a much more functional relationship between their money and their lives. With an advisor who educates clients and keeps them focused, revolutionary investors are sure to make consistent progress toward their goals.

As a revolutionary, it's important to keep a vision of your future self in mind. With strong processes like personal wealth management and the tools therein, you can find the most dynamic ways to stay on track and benefit your future self. Look around, and you'll probably find examples of who you don't want to become, as well.

Are You Ready for Today's Revolution?

Despite my optimism on the subject of a great future ahead, many media articles have called my generation an age-related disaster waiting to happen. According to them, American society won't be able to cope with millions upon millions of us doddering old souls. They portray us as a potential plague of locusts, scouring the landscape clean, leaving nothing for the generations that follow.

As you've undoubtedly discovered by now, I have a completely different prediction: I believe the rock-and-roll generation is about to launch its next revolution, changing forever the way society views life after 50 and the way people age.

The investor revolution is about much more than money. It's about investing in yourself in a way to create the best future life possible. It's about investing your time and thoughts into creating a compelling vision of your future life. Your life after 40, 50, and beyond will be different from any previous generation. The maturity of the Information Age will give you the freedom to live and work wherever and pretty much whenever you want. Information and technology will not only make you more productive, but will also improve the quality of your life in many ways.

Our generation has taken a different approach to health than those before us. We go to doctors, get knee replacements to keep running marathons, take vitamins, eat organically, and keep physically fit. Just as we've begun the revolution for health, we'll lead the revolution for wealth. Many of us believe it will be possible to feel like we're 20, 30, or even 40 years younger than previous generations did at the same age. And we're planning on doing something worthwhile with those additional years, which means we'll need to invest money in a way that will make more money instead of losing it. Sounds simple, but as you learned from this book, it may not be that simple. To get excellent results in the areas I discussed will require revolutionary breakthroughs and approaches. Traditional methods haven't produced the desired results; many will produce even worse results in the future because the environment is ever-changing.

People today have an unprecedented opportunity, not only for ourselves as individuals but for society as a whole. In the 1960s, we witnessed a cultural revolution. Now it's time for the next revolution—the investor revolution. My hope is that many people will take the action necessary to participate in this revolution. Will you be one of them?

Live a Legacy Now

A successful life often encompasses more than just the person who's living it. As a revolutionary investor, you have the opportunity to concentrate on living a legacy. That may sound unsettling at first, but it's more important to live a legacy than to leave one. Capitalize on the present while it's here, and realize that posthumous acknowledgement is nice, but you're focused on the here and now.

As most of my clients will attest, when people begin to accumulate more wealth, they become more charitable. One way to maximize your feelings of fulfillment and self-worth is to give back to important causes. This is a way of extending your success and branching out to create good for others, long after you've created good for yourself.

Bill Gates, one of the world's wealthiest individuals and a boomer, committed $24 billion of his personal wealth a few years ago to the goal of providing health care for the world's poorest children. Before making that commitment, Gates was merely a very wealthy man. After he made the commitment, he became a wealthy man who could make an enormous contribution to the world. The difference was not the wealth, but his vision of how to apply it to a bigger purpose. You may never have the financial resources of a Bill Gates, but you too can make a difference in the world—if you have a vision.

One of our clients, Susan, is passionate about being a philanthropist. She's made many charitable contributions in the past, and most were admirably devoid of her own name, but she was looking to develop a greater connection between her donations and the positive outcomes of her giving. Susan was interested in giving back to her community but was unable to find a suitable avenue to do so. She found it hard to say "no" without feeling guilty when asked for contributions. She dreaded telling a group to whom she'd donated last year that the charity wouldn't be included on her list this time around.

Susan attended a philanthropy workshop for women, where she was advised to consult with a philanthropy coach. She met with us to work through how and where she should donate her money and why. Through the process of personal wealth coaching, we reaffirmed Susan's need to feel a sense of worthiness by building a solid foundation of charitable contributions. Susan recognized her boundaries—she knew she couldn't save the world. She began to learn ways to go beyond the impersonal process of writing a check and chose to be more engaged with the lives of the people she was passionate to serve.

Within a few months, Susan found her calling. She founded a facility where unwed mothers can birth their children in a healthy and supportive environment. The facility has become somewhat of a sanctuary for young women, a safe haven of sorts. It's a healthcare option that didn't exist before Susan, and she enjoys her work greatly.

Lorene Burkhart, a noted philanthropist in central Indiana, said that many times, donors—especially women philanthropists—aren't interested in individual glory. Rather, they're intrigued by the personal processes involved, which often lead to new opportunities for educational institutions and nonprofit organizations.

"As women become more focused on the opportunities to expand their own impact, both with money and with connecting with other women, they become energized and generous," said Burkhart. "Philanthropy is turning a corner when professional women realize their potential. How they capitalize on it will require training from experts, so they don't end up with a lack of connection between their giving and their fulfillment from giving."

A lack of financial resources represents one of the worst outcomes imaginable for your life. Revolutionaries are rarely penniless and overstressed, and where many of the Wall Street titans ended isn't where you want to be headed. As with your life, a certain training process is required to help you determine where your charitable donations might go. Becoming a philanthropist may not appeal to everybody, but giving back in various ways is good for everyone, including the giver. As you march on toward absolute fulfillment, stay mindful that a truly prosperous life involves more lives than your own.

Enjoying Your Leisure Time

Ever since the Middle Ages, people have been slaves to the mechanical clock. The Industrial Age conveyed the idea that leisure time was immoral. Today, we complain of 60- or 70-hour workweeks, yet we're unable to successfully integrate our work and leisure time. Instead, we oscillate between all work and all play, living unbalanced lives.

In the future, I believe we'll create a better balance between our work and leisure time. Perhaps we'll follow the example of Wes, a friend who turned his life toward the better. At age 50, Wes was the president and chief operating officer of an auto-body paint distributing company. He'd been brought in to turn the business around, and after doing so, he started feeling a little bored. He examined the possibilities for his future life and made a radical decision. "The company's doing well, and we report record earnings," he said, "but this isn't what I want to do. And that won't change unless I take the initiative."

Wes and his wife had talked for some time about spending more time in Arizona, where their son lives. Doing some right-brain visioning, Wes realized that if he could reduce his work hours by a third, they'd be able to bring their vision to life. He let his left brain kick in and came up with a plan: "Because I'm still working for the company, doing things that need to happen every week, I can't work two months and take a month off. So what I've figured out is, I take off every Friday, every other Thursday, and one more day a month. I love that."

Wes cut back to two-thirds time, which revolutionized the workweek that was bringing him down. He used information technology to revolutionize the way he worked and as a result give him life choices he didn't have before.

I could go on and on listing revolutionary investors I've known who changed their lives for the better. As the rock-and-roll generation begins the move toward enjoying more leisure time, we'll keep pushing the bounds of traditional retirement. Some revolutionary boomer will coin a new term, and we'll soon be hearing that wonderful later state of our life called something other than just *retirement*.

As increasing numbers of rock-and-rollers decide to do everything from consult part-time to write books to start their own businesses instead of working for someone else full time, the marketplace will respond to their demand for courses, seminars, and other supportive materials to help them in their quest. We'll see more evidence that the hunger for knowledge is constantly calling.

As the investor revolution takes hold, we'll no longer have the inherent inclination to worry. We'll have too many positive ideas and innovations to look forward to. We'll be more focused on living the life that's right for us, and we won't make catastrophes out of cracks in the sidewalk.

The Future Begins Now

This isn't the first time our country has witnessed a transition between ages. But, as rock-and-rollers, it's our first and last shot at revolutionizing an age to our advantage. From the Industrial Age on, each subsequent era has become more dynamic than the one before it, creating more change than its predecessor.

Those people who didn't have the vision to see what the industrial age was ultimately going to do pitied the generation that would follow them. They felt times weren't going to be as good in the future as they may have been in the past, and the poor generations to follow would have to endure the conclusion of the age. Surely the proprietors of buggy-whip businesses fretted for their children when they saw the first automobiles buzzing around. That negative mind-set has carried over to some people today, for no justifiable reason.

Those people fail to see the solid infrastructure that the Information Age has laid. New industries and new philosophies will lead to a new level of prosperity beyond anything the inhabitants of the Industrial Age could have possibly imagined. By those primordial standards, we're all living as kings and queens, and we've probably forgotten about more of our life luxuries than Industrial Age people ever had.

We've become accustomed to convenience and living more ful-filled lives than any generation before us. Despite this, the rock-and-roll generation is aware that we're not as complacent with our lives as we could be. We may have the castle, but we want the king-dom, too. As a result, our generation is beginning to focus more on a life-work balance—creating a source of lasting fulfillment—and how to utilize the available technology and information to buttress our lives.

The generations now rising in the wake of the rock-and-roll generation weren't tainted with old-model traditions, for the most part. The X and Y generations have seen less of the workaday liveli-hoods we rock-and-rollers saw our parents live; they've grown up with computers and a dynamic world. They expect customization. The younger crowds are less apt to spend their lives chasing pension plans and retirement gift watches. They're beginning to recognize us as trailblazers—as career-focused individuals who are passion-ate about progressing after our conventional working years—and they're gladly following our path.

> **Generation X** generally refers to those born between 1961 and 1981. **Generation Y** includes those born between 1977 and 2003 and is just as large a generation as the baby boomers.

Many people who are filling today's technology needs are younger than the average baby boomer. Think about that—the ris-ing innovators of tomorrow could be your kids. They're watching the boomer mass as it lunges through the decades, having long since figured out that computers are the wave of the future. By develop-ing technologies to suit the massive need, they've matched the left-brain technical aspects of developing things like computer programs and marvelous smart phones with the initial creative ideas of those products. Their revolution lies in bridging conceptual ideas with tangible innovations and then selling it all to us. They're the first generation to harness a whole-brain world.

The revolution is only the beginning of the real change. It all takes a while. The upcoming generations will do very well because they'll see the revolution through its early stage and pick the fruits of its maturity. They'll reap the benefits resulting from their ability to create processes that integrate informational tools to deal with an ever more dynamic world. The result will be customization of what we need and the ability to use it to improve the quality of our lives. They'll do this because we've shown them how.

Take Action—Today!

We started this book with Bob Dylan, and we'll finish it with him, too. Some believe he deserves to be called the Shakespeare of our generation. As was the case 40 years ago, the times are certainly a-changin'. The younger generations will have to adapt far less to these changes than we have done, because we've cleared a remarkable path already.

The baby boomers have had it easy in comparison to the generation preceding us, the Greatest Generation, whose ability to endure marks their place in American history. Thinking back to the changes my grandmother witnessed boggles my mind. In her youth, she lived on a farm and rode a horse from place to place, because that was the most reliable means of transportation. A few years before she died, NASA put a man on the moon. I sit back sometimes, entwine my hands behind my head, and think about that. I'm baffled by the drastic, world-changing transformations that grew to maturity during her lifetime, not to mention my life. Since 1900, the human race has come many miles, and it's poised to go many more.

In just 60 years, a revolution flipped the establishment upside down, spanning the simplified days of horse-drawn carriages to the dynamic times of outer-space voyages. Consider this another 1900. We're just beginning. The revolution is just taking hold. With the maturity of the Information Age, the twenty-first century will be a time in which every person becomes their own entity, and everything from their soy lattes to their dreams of idyllic livelihoods will be customized for them. For you. For the revolutionary investors. For the individuals of our time who take action, because no revolution ever occurs on its own. It won't just happen—we need to embrace the change, to shake things up as we've been doing for decades. This will be an incredible era, and it's chanting at our doorstep, urging us to join in.

Challenge yourself to think differently. Don't settle for the ideals of a faltering paradigm. Don't be force-fed tradition when you know you can do better. Your life doesn't have to be anchored by a 40-, 50-, or even 60-hour workweek. Your job doesn't have to be the price you pay to enjoy time away from work. Don't watch the clock and urge your life to tick away, and don't settle for some eternal weekend of leisure, either. Focus instead on living the most rewarding, active, fulfilling life you can possibly imagine, and then go after it. You have tools at your disposal that past generations couldn't begin to conceptualize, which are like the bayonets of our own Napoleonic movement.

Think of the big deals of the past hundred years, the innovations that created a worldwide phenomenon. The unsinkable Titanic, radio, television, the automobile, the wireless telephone—all amazing innovations that we take for granted today. Information and technology are next in line. They're earmarked to be passé, to be a given, like the water we no longer pull from a well. Where will we be then, when a critical mass of people is looking way beyond these archaic concepts?

It all comes back to finding out what we truly want—and what we want is something new. Tradition can be a good thing. Being from the Midwest, I'm probably more into tradition as it relates to family and history than many people in America. I'll also say that traditional thinking can lead to no thinking at all and can get in the way of advancing and improving our lives for the better. Let's do away with the word *tradition*. Let's be open-minded, thinking outside the box. Let's get creative and quick and not be locked in the old traditional model, which is all but obsolete. Let's begin to think conceptually, to be innovative and not afraid of change. Let's sift through the pollution to find the knowledge we need—the truth without the fat. Technology is only expanding, not shrinking, and our ability to survive depends on our skill in grasping it. Use it to find the right process, one that deals with an increasingly dynamic environment and numberless tools—a process that disposes of second-rate products and embraces a futuristic blueprint.

The right process expands the definitions of wealth and success. The time to choose our direction is now, and the right answers are out there, waiting. The rock-and-roll generation cut our teeth on change, but we let the big ideas slip away as we eased into a role of complacency. It's time to transform the creaking machinery of yesteryear, because we as revolutionaries demand better. It's time to rock and roll again. Let the investor revolution begin!

Appendix

The Wealth Management Benchmark®

We use a more extensive, computerized version of the Wealth Management Benchmark (WMB) in our practice. Here is an abbreviated form of the WMB so that you can see what is involved in the process.

In the following exercise, you'll find six categories or critical life areas, with four statements under each one. For each statement, you'll be asked to do three things:

1. *Determine the issue's importance.* If it's important to you, place a check mark in the first column. If the issue isn't important, leave the column blank.

2. *Determine the issue's completeness.* If the issue is incomplete and needs your attention, place a check mark in the second column. If the issue has been completed, leave the column blank.

3. *Determine a time frame for completion.* If you placed check marks in the first and second columns (meaning the issue is important and needs to be completed), insert a completion time in the third column. Write "3" if you want to complete the issue in the next three months, "6" if you want to complete it within four to six months, or "12" if you intend to complete it within the next seven to twelve months.

Let's go through the first Net Worth & Cash Management issue together. It says, "Create a net worth and cash flow statement." Is doing that important to you? Do you think it would be a good idea to spend some time developing a net worth and cash flow statement? If so, place a check mark in the first column.

Next, what's your level of completeness in this issue? Let's say you've thought about it a little but you haven't taken any action. In that case, place a check mark in the second column.

Finally, what's your time frame for completion? Let's say you'd be willing to do it within the next six months, but you're busy right now and know it will be at least four months before you'll have the time. In that case, write "6" in the last column.

Go ahead and complete the exercise, and then we'll take the final steps.

Now, look at the Timing column. On a separate sheet of paper, list the issues to which you assigned a time frame, in order of priority. In other words, start with all the 3 issues, then all the 6 issues, and finally all the 12 issues. The result is your action plan. Post this list where you can see it often, and commit to meeting the deadlines you've set. Then, you can work with your advisors to tackle each issue, determine an optimum schedule for reviewing and evaluating your progress, and establish the best ways to continue fine-tuning your individualized personal wealth management strategy. Before you leave this exercise, choose two items from your action plan and commit to a date for getting them done.

Please remember, this exercise is offered just to give you a taste of the experience. The actual Wealth Management Benchmark is much more extensive, and coaching is an important part of the process.

	Importance	Needs Completion	Timing 3 (1–3 mos.) 6 (4–6 mos.) 12 (7–12 mos.)
Net Worth & Cash Management			
1. Create a net worth and cash flow statement.			
2. Establish a method to track your cash flow and expenses.			
3. Confirm that any existing debt is tax efficient and represents a reasonable percentage of your assets.			
4. Confirm that all tax-advantaged employee benefits (such as 401(k) and deferred compensation) are being maximized.			
Investment Planning			
1. Discuss your overall investment philosophy and create an Investment Policy Statement (IPS).			
2. Confirm diversification among and within different investment classes.			
3. Confirm that you own the highest quality securities.			
4. Ensure that *all* your financial assets are following the directives of your IPS.			

	Importance	Needs Completion	Timing 3 (1–3 mos.) 6 (4–6 mos.) 12 (7–12 mos.)
Retirement Planning			
1. Explore the possibilities of continued employment or other opportunities for generating income.			
2. Complete a retirement planning analysis six months prior to any career transition.			
3. Review the process for generating cash flow at retirement.			
4. Evaluate retirement accounts that need to be established.			
Estate & Legacy Planning			
1. Discuss your estate and legacy philosophy with an estate planning advisor.			
2. Create a detailed outline of your objectives.			
3. Establish trusts, determine trust funding, and draft wills and all necessary related documents.			
4. With family members, discuss decision-making in case of incapacitation, life support, and final wishes.			

	Importance	Needs Completion	Timing 3 (1–3 mos.) 6 (4–6 mos.) 12 (7–12 mos.)
Life Planning			
1. Create a compelling vision of your future life.			
2. Complete a Quality of Life™ assessment.			
3. Create a plan to fulfill your vision.			
4. Get an annual physical exam, and take the steps recommended by your qualifed health practitioner to enhance your vitality.			
Asset & Income Protection			
1. Confirm that your insurance (auto, property, casualty, personal liability, and so on) is appropriate and cost effective.			
2. Identify the amount of life insurance necessary to meet your family's needs in the event of a sudden death, and develop a life insurance plan.			
3. Complete a home inventory, including listing bequests of personal property.			
4. Analyze and make decisions regarding long-term care.			

Bibliography

The American Heritage Dictionary of the English Language, 4th ed., s.v. "cognitive dissonance," "revolution."

Armstrong, Frank. *The Informed Investor*. American Management Association, 2003.

Beach, David M. "Jay Gould: The Greatest Financier and the Most Powerful Robber Baron in American History." *Scripophily* (June 1995).

Brain, Marshall. "How Gnutella Works." HowStuffWorks. http://computer.howstuffworks.com/file-sharing.htm/printable (accessed November 13, 2006).

Brinson, Gary P., L. Randolph Hood, and Gilbert Beebower. "Determinants of Portfolio Performance." *Financial Analysts Journal* (July–August 1986).

Brown, S. Kathi. "Staying Ahead of the Curve 2003: The AARP Working in Retirement Study." AARP (2003). http://www.aarp. org/money/careers/employerresourcecenter/trends/a2004-08-02-curve2003.html (accessed October 25, 2006).

Bryan, Michael, Bruce Champ, and Jennifer Ransom. "Who Is That Guy on the $10 Bill?" Federal Reserve Bank of Cleveland. http://www.clevelandfed.org/Research/Com2000/0600.htm (accessed October 23, 2006).

Dent, Harry S. Jr. *The Great Boom Ahead: Your Guide to Personal & Business Profit in the New Era of Prosperity*. New York: Hyperion, 1993.

Digital Insurrection. "Tivo Introduction." http://pvr.digitalinsurrection.com/tivo/tivo_intro.php (accessed October 23, 2006).

Elmiger, Gregory and Steve S. Kim. *RiskGrade Your Investments: Measure Your Risk and Create Wealth*. New Jersey: John Wiley & Sons, Inc., 2003.

Flamme, Karen. "1995 Annual Report: A Brief History of Our Nation's Paper Money." Federal Reserve Bank of San Francisco. http://www.frbsf.org/publications/federalreserve/annual/1995/history.html (accessed October 23, 2006).

Foner, Eric, and John A. Garraty, ed. *The Reader's Companion to American History*. New York: Houghton Mifflin Company, 1991.

Friedman, Jack P. *Dictionary of Business Terms*. Barron's Educational Series, 2000.

Gaberlavage, George, Sharon Hermanson, Christopher Baker, Kellie Kim-Sung, Neal Walters, Mitja Ng-Baumhackl, and Ann McLarty Jackson. "Beyond 50.04: A Report to the Nation on Consumers in the Marketplace." AARP, May 2004. http://www.aarp.org/research/reference/agingtrends/aresearch-import-860.html (accessed October 25, 2006).

Gibson, Roger C. *Asset Allocation: Balancing Financial Risk*. New York: McGraw-Hill, 2000.

Hardin, Thomas L. *Never Too Old to Rock and Roll: Life After 50— The Best Years Yet*. With Gail Fink. Zionsville, IN: Canterbury Publishing Group, 2005.

Holley, Hana. "Retirement Planning Survey Among U.S. Adults Age 40 and Older." AARP, May 2006. http://www.aarp.org/research/financial/retirementsaving/ret_planning.html (accessed October 25, 2006).

Investopedia. http://www.investopedia.com/.

InvestorWords. http://www.investorwords.com/.

Moeller, Steve. *Effort-Less Marketing for Financial Advisors*. Tustin, CA: American Business Visions, 1999.

Mulvey, John M. "Essential Portfolio Theory." White paper. Rydex Investments, May 2005.

National Oceanic and Atmospheric Administration. "1974 Tornado Outbreak." http://www.publicaffairs.noaa.gov/storms/ (accessed October 25, 2006).

Officer, Lawrence H. and Samuel H. Williamson, "Purchasing Power of Money in the United States from 1774 to 2005." MeasuringWorth.com, August 2006. http://www. measuringworth.com/ppowerus/ (accessed October 24, 2006).

Schwartz, Barry. *The Paradox of Choice: Why More Is Less*. Ecco, 2004.

Siegel, Jeremy J. *The Future for Investors: Why the Tried and the True Triumph Over the Bold and the New*. New York: Crown Business, 2005.

———. *Stocks for the Long Run: The Definitive Guide to Financial Market Returns and Long-Term Investment Strategies*. New York: McGraw-Hill, 1998.

TD Ameritrade. "What You Need to Know About Financial Advice." 2006. http://www.tdainstitutional.com/advisoreducation/media/ FinancialAdvice.pdf (accessed October 25, 2006).

TD Ameritrade. "Investor Perception Study 2006." 2006. http://www.tdainstitutional.com/advisoreducation/media/ InvestorPerceptionStudy.pdf (accessed October 25, 2006).

Unilever Food & Health Research Institute. "Healthy for Longer: Scientific and Communication Issues Relevant to Consumer Health and Vitality." Vlaardingen, The Netherlands: Unilever Food & Health Research Institute, 2005.

Warshow, Robert Irving. *The Story of Wall Street*. New York: Greenberg Publisher, 1931.

Wikipedia contributors. "Cultural movement." Wikipedia, The Free Encyclopedia. http://en.wikipedia.org/wiki/Cultural_movement (accessed October 26, 2006).

Glossary

Active management: An investment strategy involving ongoing buying and selling actions by the investor. Active investors purchase investments and continuously monitor their activity in order to exploit profitable conditions. Investors believe it's possible to profit from the stock market through any number of strategies that identify undervalued securities.

Age: A period in the history of humankind marked by a distinctive characteristic or achievement.

Analysis paralysis: An informal phrase applied to the condition when the opportunity cost of decision analysis exceeds the benefits.

Annuities: Investment product in which a series of fixed payments is paid to the investor at regular intervals over the specified period of the annuity.

Asset: A resource having economic value that an individual, corporation, or country owns or controls with the expectation that it will provide future benefit.

Asset allocation: The process of dividing a portfolio among major asset classes such as stocks, bonds, and cash.

Boom: A period of higher-than-average growth in the stock market, economy, or other sector. The term refers to explosive growth.

Certified Financial Planner™ (CFP®): A financial advisor who takes extensive exams in the areas of financial planning, taxes, insurance, estate planning, and retirement and also completes continuing education programs each year to maintain certification status.

Certified Investment Management Consultant (CIMC): An investment professional who has completed extensive course work and passed NASD proctored examinations for Levels I and II of the Institute for Certified Investment Management Consultants' course. The CIMC must also meet requirements related to experience in consulting and managed accounts, adhere to a code of ethics, and meet continuing education requirements.

Chartered Financial Analyst® (CFA®): A professional designation that measures the competence and integrity of financial analysts. The analyst is required to pass three levels of exams covering areas such as accounting, economics, ethics, money management, and security analysis, and must have a minimum of three years of investment/financial experience.

Chartered Financial Consultant (ChFC): A financial professional who has completed a course which includes the courses for CFP certification and builds on that knowledge with classes in estate, retirement, and in-depth financial planning applications. Certification requires three years of full-time business experience and continuing education.

Chartered Market Technician (CMT): A premier designation in technical market analysis, which includes three levels of testing and takes three to five years to complete. The CMT is required to be bound by a code of ethics.

Cognitive dissonance: The condition of conflict or anxiety resulting from inconsistency between your beliefs and your actions, such as believing that smoking is harmful but continuing to do it.

Conceptual age: A period characterized by high-concept and high-touch resulting from a focus on the big-picture capabilities of right-brained people.

Consults program: An investment program in which a consultant structures a portfolio, generally using outside money managers/brokers.

Correlation: A statistical measure of how two securities move in relation to each other.

Customize: To modify or build according to individual or personal specifications or preference.

Customized portfolio management: The process of aligning a client's investment portfolio to the client's clearly defined goals and objectives.

Diversification: Holding a collection of independent assets in order to reduce overall risk.

Diversification effect: The impact that the inclusion of a particular asset class or security has on the volatility and return characteristics of the overall portfolio.

Dow Jones Industrial Average (DJIA): A price-weighted average of thirty significant stocks traded on the New York Stock Exchange and the Nasdaq. Often referred to as "the Dow," the DJIA is the oldest index in the world.

Efficient market theory: An economic theory that states that there is a relationship between risk, or price fluctuation, and return. More fluctuation should justify a higher rate of return, but it takes a longer amount of time to reach an average expected return. Conversely, with only a little fluctuation, the return will be less but will be more predictable.

Efficient portfolio: A portfolio that earns the highest return with the least amount of volatility.

Equity-risk premium: The higher rate of return that comes from taking higher risk.

Exchange-traded fund (ETF): A security that tracks an index, a commodity, or a basket of assets like an index fund, but trades like a stock on an exchange, thus experiencing price changes throughout the day as it's bought and sold. Such a fund provides the diversification of an index fund as well as the ability to sell short, buy on margin, and purchase as little as one share. Another advantage is that the expense ratios for most ETFs are lower than those of the average mutual fund. Buying and selling ETFs results in the same trading costs as with any security.

Financial planner: A generalist who helps individuals and corporations meet their long-term financial objectives by analyzing the client's status and setting a program to achieve those goals.

Fluctuations: The ups and downs of a market.

Free market theory: An economic principle, first postulated by Adam Smith, holding that the greatest benefit to a society is brought about by individuals acting freely in a competitive marketplace in the pursuit of their own self interest.

Fundamental analysis: A method of analyzing a security by using financial, economic, quantitative, and qualitative indicators to determine the intrinsic value. Fundamental analysts study everything that can impact the security's value, from macroeconomic factors (such as the overall economy and industry conditions) to individually specific factors (such as the financial condition and management of companies).

Generation X: Generally refers to those born between 1961 and 1981.

Generation Y: Includes those born between 1977 and 2003 and is just as large a generation as the baby boomers.

Google: A well-known Web search engine that indexes billions of Web pages and provides a free service that searches this index in less than a second.

Googol: A number that is equal to 1 followed by 100 zeros, or 10^{100}.

Greatest Generation: Derived from the title of a best-selling book by Tom Brokaw, and generally assumed to mean those born in the United States from about 1911 through 1924. People from this generation are the parents of the majority of the baby boomers; they fought during World War II (and many fought again in the Korean War) and went on to rebuild the world's industries in the following years.

Index: A statistical measure of change in an economy or a securities market. In the case of financial markets, an index is essentially an imaginary portfolio of securities representing a particular market or a portion of it. Each index has its own calculation methodology and is usually expressed in terms of a change from a base value. Thus, the percentage change is more important than the actual numeric value. For example, knowing that a stock exchange is at, say, 12,000 doesn't tell you much. However, knowing that the index has risen 10 percent over the last year to 12,000 gives a much better demonstration of performance.

Index fund: A portfolio of investments that is weighted the same as a stock-exchange index in order to mirror its performance. Investing in an index fund is a form of passive investing. The primary advantage to such a strategy is the lower management expense ratio on an index fund.

Industrial Age: A period in the eighteenth and nineteenth centuries marking the introduction of mass production, improved transportation, technological progress, and the industrial factory system.

Information Age: The period beginning around 1970 and noted for the abundant publication, consumption, and manipulation of information, especially on computers and computer networks.

Information anxiety: Disquiet "produced by the ever-widening gap between what we understand and what we think we should understand. It's the black hole between data and knowledge, and it happens when information doesn't tell us what we want to or need to know." —Richard Saul Wurman

Investment management consultant: A financial advisor who typically structures a client's portfolio using outside money managers/brokers or mutual funds. Such a person is sometimes called a "manager of the managers" or the manager of a broker consults program.

Investment Policy Statement (IPS): A document that outlines investment guidelines and procedures for portfolio management for a specific client.

Investor: For the purposes of this book, anyone who has money invested. This term does not refer to a professional who invests money for other people.

Investor revolution: A movement among progressive-thinking individuals to manage investment securities, tools, and information to fit an ever-changing market environment. The result is a customized dynamic process that connects their money to peoples' lives and achieves lifelong successful performance.

Invisible hand: A natural phenomenon that guides free markets and capitalism through competition for scarce resources.

Leverage: The use of various financial instruments or borrowed capital to increase the potential return of an investment. It can be created through options, futures, margin, and other instruments.

Life visioning: A process that can help you create a compelling vision of your future life, discover a vision of possibilities, and outline the goals to achieve it.

Limited customization: The process of choosing from a set list of available mass-produced options that best meet your need.

Liquidity: The ability to convert an asset to cash quickly.

Market timing: The process of attempting to predict future market directions, and investing based on those predictions. The goal is to be in the market when it goes up and out when it goes down.

Modern portfolio theory: The theory that a higher portfolio return is possible with lower portfolio fluctuation if the investments in the portfolio work together. One of the basics behind this theory is the attempt to create an efficient portfolio, one that earns the highest return with the least amount of volatility.

Mutual fund: A security that gives investors access to a portfolio of equities, bonds, and other securities. Each shareholder participates in the gain or loss of the fund. Shares are issued and can be redeemed as needed.

Nasdaq: The world's first electronic stock market. This computer-ized system facilitates trading and provides price quotations on some 5,000 of the more actively traded over-the-counter stocks. Unlike the New York Stock Exchange and the American Stock Exchange, the Nasdaq doesn't have a physical trading floor that brings buyers and sellers together; all trading is done over a network of computers and telephones.

New York Stock Exchange (NYSE): The largest stock exchange in the US. It uses traders rather than computers to make trades.

Passive management: An investment strategy involving limited ongoing buying and selling actions. Passive investors purchase investments with the intention of long-term appreciation and lim-ited maintenance. Followers of passive management believe in the efficient market hypothesis, which states that at all times, markets incorporate and reflect all information, so stock-picking is futile. As a result, the best investing strategy is to invest in an index fund in order to mirror a market index and not attempt to beat the mar-ket.

Personal wealth: A measure of wealth that includes aspects beyond money and tangibles, such as relationships, health, and a vision of the future.

Personal wealth coach: A financial professional who helps people envision, monitor, and achieve maximum fulfillment from both their tangible and intangible wealth. The coach accomplishes these important goals by focusing on two key components: financial/investment services and personal life issues.

Personal wealth management: A unique process for helping people achieve and manage total wealth and abundance in all their forms. It can be broken down into two critical areas: personal wealth coach-ing and customized portfolio management.

Portfolio manager (institutional): The person with the discretion to buy and sell securities on behalf of a client in the implementation of the client's investment strategy. The manager is generally paid a fee based on the dollar value of the assets managed.

Portfolio manager (revolutionary): A financial professional who plays an educational and consultative role, teaching clients about the fundamentals of investing, customizing and managing the portfolio based on the clients' specific objectives and risk parameters, and counseling them through difficult periods in the market.

Portfolio Thermostat™: An investment technique that utilizes RiskGrades® to manage fluctuations within a specific investor's predetermined comfort or tolerance range.

Quality of Life™ index: An assessment of how aligned a client is with six happiness factors and how satisfied the client is with life.

Reticular activating system: A network of structures, including the brain stem, medulla, thalamus, and nerve pathways, which function together to produce and maintain arousal.

Reverse fund: A mutual fund that seeks to provide investment results that inversely correspond to the performance of the market (often a specified market index).

Revolution: A sudden or momentous change in a situation.

Risk: Uncertainty, or exposure to a chance of loss.

RiskGrade®: An indicator of market risk that allows for a comparison of investment risk across all asset classes, regions, and currencies, and that varies over time to reflect asset specific information (such as the price of a stock reacting to an earnings release) and general market conditions.

Robber baron: One of the American industrial or financial magnates of the late nineteenth century who became wealthy by unethical means, such as questionable stock-market operations and exploitation of labor.

Sector: A distinct subset of a market whose components share similar characteristics. Stocks are often grouped into different sectors depending on the companies' businesses. Standard & Poor's breaks the market into eleven sectors: utilities, consumer staples, transportation, technology, health care, financial, energy, consumer cyclicals, basic materials, capital goods, and communications services.

Securities and Exchange Commission (SEC): The agency charged with administering federal securities laws in the U.S. The SEC oversees the key participants in the securities world, including securities exchanges, securities brokers and dealers, investment advisors, and mutual funds. The SEC is concerned primarily with promoting the disclosure of important market-related information, maintaining fair dealing, and protecting against fraud.

Standard and Poor's 500 (S&P 500): Five hundred companies selected by the S&P Index Committee, a team of analysts and economists at Standard and Poor's, for their market size, liquidity, and industry grouping. This list is meant to reflect the risk/return of U.S. large-cap stocks as a whole. Standard and Poor's is a financial services company that rates stocks and corporate and municipal bonds according to risk profiles.

Standard & Poor's 500 index (S&P 500 index): An index consisting of the 500 stocks in the S&P 500. The S&P 500 index is designed to be a leading indicator of U.S. equities. The Dow Jones Industrial Average (DJIA) was at one time the most renowned index for U.S. stocks, but because the DJIA contains only 30 companies, most people agree that the S&P 500 is a better representation of the U.S. market.

Standard deviation: A statistical measure of the historical volatility of a mutual fund or portfolio.

Standardize: To bring to or make of an established standard size, weight, quality, strength, or the like.

Stockbroker or broker: An agent (typically a registered representative of a NYSE firm) who charges a commission for executing buy and sell orders submitted by an investor. A broker is prohibited from charging a fee for advice while trading.

Style-specific: An investment approach that selects securities or funds of a certain type.

Style-specific investment manager: A manager who invests in just one style of investments, such as growth stocks, value stocks, contrarian stocks, and so on, or mutual funds with a very specific investment focus.

Systematic/market-related risk: The risk inherent to the entire market or entire market segment. This is undiversifiable risk.

Technical analysis: A method of evaluating securities by analyzing statistics generated by market activity, such as past prices and volume. Technical analysts don't attempt to measure a security's intrinsic value, but instead use charts and other tools to identify patterns that can suggest future activity.

True customization: An approach that requires a human element to execute the process of combining the available choices with the individual need to achieve a very specific result.

Unsystematic/stock-specific risk: Risk that affects a small number of stocks. For example, news that is specific to a small number of stocks, such as a sudden strike by the employees of a company you have shares in, is considered to be unsystematic risk.

Variance: A measure of the dispersion of a set of data points around their mean value. Variance is a mathematical expectation of the average squared deviations from the mean. Variance measures the variability or volatility from an average. Volatility is a measure of risk, so this statistic can help determine the risk an investor might take on when purchasing a specific security.

Volatility: The relative rate at which the price of a stock or security moves up and down. If the price of a stock moves up and down rapidly over short time periods, it has high volatility. If the price almost never changes, it has low volatility.

Wealth Management Benchmark® (WMB): An ongoing process that evolved from financial planning and, unlike traditional financial planning, covers all areas of personal wealth. It can be administered by either a personal wealth coach or a portfolio manager. The process begins by addressing specific issues in six personal wealth management categories: Net Worth and Cash Management, Investment Planning, Retirement Planning, Estate and Legacy Planning, Life Planning, and Asset and Income Protection.

Wrap fee: A flat quarterly or annual fee charged by a brokerage to manage a portfolio. This fee includes trading costs, administrative fees, commissions, and management expenses.

Index

What is the single most important question you have about how the investor revolution affects you?

Tom invites you to send him your questions at **tom@canterburygroup.com** or visit Canterbury Group's web site at **www.CanterburyGroup.com**, where you will also get dynamic and current content from the author such as:

- Tom's blog
- Tom's *Tip of the Week* (register online to receive this weekly)
- Articles and recommended reading
- *Frequently Asked Questions* about Tom's process
- Tom's upcoming seminars, events, and appearances
- Information about Tom's firm *Canterbury Investment Management*

TOM HARDIN offers keynotes, seminars, and workshops for individuals, groups, and professional organizations, based on either *Investor Revolution!* or his first book, *Never Too Old to Rock and Roll*. He can also customize his speaking engagements to meet your needs. Some examples of his seminar topics are:

- Revolutionary Investment Management for the 21st Century
- The Future for Baby Boomers and the Rock and Roll Generation
- Understanding Technical Market Analysis
- Global Investment Management
  - The Psychology of Money and Investing
  - Fundamentals of Investing and Portfolio Management

Contact the author at:

TOM HARDIN, Canterbury Group
23 East Cedar Street, Zionsville, IN 46077
317-732-2075 Fax: 317-873-8123
E-mail: tom@canterburygroup.com

www.CanterburyGroup.com